DinOsauR HEART TRANS- PLANTS

R. ROBERT CUENI

DINOSAUR HEART TRANS- PLANTS

RENEWING MAINLINE CONGREGATIONS

Abingdon Press
Nashville

DINOSAUR HEART TRANSPLANTS
RENEWING MAINLINE CONGREGATIONS

Copyright © 2000 by Abingdon Press

This book is printed on recycled, acid-free, elemental-chlorine–free paper.

Library of Congress Cataloging-in-Publication Data

Cueni, R. Robert.
Dinosaur heart transplants : renewing mainline congregations / R. Robert Cueni.
p. cm.
ISBN 0-687-08466-0 (alk. paper)
1. Church renewal. I. Title.

BV600.2.C755 2000
250—dc21   99-047608

00 01 02 03 04 05 06 07 08 09—10 9 8 7 6 5 4 3 2 1

MANUFACTURED IN THE UNITED STATES OF AMERICA

To the twins:
Annika Elaine and Elizabeth Jane—
*the next chapter
in our family story*

CONTENTS

IT'S THE NAME OF THE NEIGHBORHOOD

Country Club Christian Church
(Disciples of Christ)

Kansas City, Missouri

A few years ago, the *Chicago Tribune* ran a list of funny church names. The writer thought the name of Lover's Lane United Methodist Church in Dallas, Texas, to be the most humorous, and the name of Country Club Christian Church in Kansas City, the congregation I serve as senior minister, to be a close second. What that *Tribune* columnist did not consider, and what I am quick to inform those unfamiliar with Kansas City, is that "Country Club" identifies the neighborhood, not our mission statement. In the early 1920s, this congregation purchased land on Ward Parkway, a soon-to-be paved boulevard, in the newly plotted subdivision named for the nearby Kansas City Country Club.

With only a handful of members, they called fifty-eight-year-old George Hamilton Combs to be founding pastor. During Combs's two-decade ministry, the congregation grew from a committee to over two thousand members. In 1926, the sanctuary for a magnificent Gothic building was designed to seat nearly nine hundred people. At the time, the congregation had fewer than three hundred members, and only a scattering of homes dotted the neighborhood.

What a testimony to the vision of the people and their leader! They intended to be a large, strong church.

Over the next few decades, the Country Club District became the leading residential neighborhood of the city and Country Club Christian Church, the place where many of the city's leading citizens belonged. A recent history of Kansas City claims that, unlike in many churches, the lay leaders of this congregation have always been more prominent than the clergy.[1] As one of those ministers, I can confirm the accuracy of the statement.

By 1948, membership had grown to three thousand members, and weekly worship attendance hovered around nine hundred. The neighborhood and the church then stopped growing. From the time of the Truman administration, the congregation has been on a plateau. For five decades, membership and worship attendance varied little. What a remarkable achievement. How incredible that any organization sustain itself, at the same level, for five decades. That takes enormous effort.

On the other hand, how easy for the membership to take this health and well-being for granted. Few congregants remember when things differed from the present. The choir program, launched in the 1940s, still ranks with the best in the city. A Sunday school class recently celebrated its sixtieth anniversary. Each week more than fifty senior members gather with the same church friends they have known all their adult lives. The neighborhood seldom gets a new house, but it remains lovely and viable. Country Club Christian Church's cathedral-like building, its location, and its reputation ensure a steady stream of visitors. The average pew sitter feels wrapped in perpetual security: "Our church will be as it always has been."

What It Takes to Renew a Mainline Congregation

Dorothy awakened from the ride on the tornado in the land of munchkins, wicked witches, and the wizard of Oz. In a flash, she stated the obvious. She said to her little dog, "Toto, we are not in Kansas anymore."

For more than thirty years, I have pastored congregations of the Christian Church (Disciples of Christ), a mainline Protestant denomination. In this time the American ecclesiastical landscape has become as unfamiliar as the land of Oz. After a generation of downward spiral in numbers and influence, as well as tornado-like social change, the denominations that once dwelt in the center have centrifuged to the margins. No longer confident to call ourselves the "mainlines," we struggle with the moniker "oldline." Many individual faith communities have marched in lockstep with their denomination on the road to decline. As a young seminarian, I admired the ministries of certain large congregations. I looked to these tall-steeple churches as leaders in mission and ministry. They set the pace and supplied the denominational leadership. Today, many of those churches have closed. Others struggle as mere shadows of their former selves. In church gatherings, whispering voices discuss them as "dinosaurs that once dominated the landscape."

Perhaps because I admired them as a young minister, I set a career path to become the senior minister of a tall-steeple church. That goal has been achieved. Most days I give thanks for God's grace. I must admit, however, sometimes I am reminded of the non-biblical proverb: "Be careful for what you pray. You might get it."

Past Performance Does Not Ensure Future Success

When I came to Country Club Christian Church in November 1991, the congregation operated much as it had since the 1950s and continued as a "Sunday morning church" dependent on pulpit power and quality classical music. Weekday programs and spiritual growth opportunities were limited. More than traditional and unchanged, the order of worship was considered unchangeable. For more than three decades, the Sunday morning bulletin ordered the same elements of worship in the same way, worded announcements the same way, and displayed on the paper the same typeface.

Discussions of a fifty-year plateau, I soon learned, were more misleading than comforting. Demographically, the congregation grew older. The main 11:00 A.M. worship service appeared as an ocean of gray hair. Evangelism records revealed that eight hundred fewer people joined the church in the 1980s than in the 1960s. A far smaller group was available to take the place of the older generation as they moved their membership to the Church Triumphant. The reality became obvious: We were likely to begin a significant decline in the next several years.

As cracks appeared in the plateau maintenance program, nationally prominent, prophetic voices began to speak of a coming "sea change." As I understood the message, the modern world gasps for its last breath as the postmodern world emerges. The continuing secularizing of American culture renders it progressively unfriendly to Christianity. The twenty-first-century American church will operate on a mission field as alien to the gospel as first-century Rome was. Local congregations, these prophets insist, must let go of their 1960s ways and develop a ministry appropriate to radically different circumstances.

14

Efforts to spread this message at Country Club Christian were met with resistance. In response to the claim that "times are changing," one older member insisted that 1952 was a wonderful time and that hard work could bring it back. Eventually, the message got through and necessary changes were instituted. The "primarily a Sunday morning worship service" model for doing and being was transformed into the programmatic style of "the seven-day-a-week church." Educational and spiritual-growth opportunities expanded enormously. We introduced intentional efforts to reach younger families. Worship services were made more flexible and participatory. These efforts started to pay off. A younger generation is finding its place in the pews. We still have three thousand members and average nearly nine hundred in attendance at three morning worship services, but we are not as "gray" as we used to be. The congregation has a sense of hopeful renewal and vitality. Thanks be to God's grace.

But Is It Enough?

"Are we doing everything necessary to put this congregation on a path to a strong future? Have we contented ourselves with fine-tuning adjustments when we need to be making a paradigmatic shift of cosmic proportions?" Those questions can bring me out of a sound sleep.

Some people claim that the survival of every mainline Protestant congregation depends on making radical, not minor, changes. To flourish, it is claimed, the church of the twenty-first century must be driven by the consumers who want the church to be and do things that greatly differ from the present. This commonly translates into a call to follow the lead of the evangelical megachurches.

The congregation of Country Club Christian Church might be compared to a dinosaur—a very traditional, large, mainline, urban church where little has changed in a half century. To be healthy into the future, must we replace the pipe organ with a rock band? Must we cease using the hymnal and commence singing praise choruses projected on large screens dropped in front of the stained-glass windows? If we expect a sufficient number of the next generation to find its way into the pews, must the sermon be outlined on printed bulletin inserts? Must the homily be delivered either from the center aisle or from behind a clear fiberglass pulpit? Must theology be harmonized with the religious right?

These claims are debated in ecclesiastical circles. Are they true? If so, I fear the congregation I serve will go the way of the Brontosaurus. Our folks do not take easily to the casual informality of contemporary worship. Historically, this congregation contends that "dignity" should be on the list of the "fruit of the Spirit." Consequently, the members expect a robed choir and a preaching minister who remains stationary behind an opaque pulpit. When attempted, praise choruses elicit more objection than encouragement. Although the congregation claims a love of all religious music, many members assume that means "from the greatest works of Bach right down to the lesser works of Bach." Because the congregation's mission and ministry continue at the level of a generation ago, people see little need for radical change.

As the lead pastor, I have a responsibility. If the future depends on doing things differently, the people must be told. With the right information, their love for the church will, I pray, move them to act accordingly. However, it will take strong evidence to convince this group to depart radically from their traditional ways of being and doing. Where does one get the facts?

Study Mainline Tall-Steeple Congregations

With the assistance of a grant from the Louisville Institute, I planned a three-month summer sabbatical to study how large, mainline congregations renew for mission and ministry. I wanted to know how many adapt to the consumer-driven expectations of the present age. Does renewal come by offering contemporary worship experiences? Do renewed congregations organize their community's spiritual life around small group ministries? How critical is a vital surrounding neighborhood? Does the building make a difference? Is renewal simply a matter of leadership?

I limited the study to congregations similar to Country Club Christian Church.

1. *Mainline.* Evangelical congregations, I believe, do things differently.

2. *Tall steeple.* Generally, I wanted to look at congregations averaging more than seven hundred in worship. However, I made exceptions to include the ways different denominations defined that expression.

3. *Older* (a tall steeple for at least forty years). I assumed churches renew into the next generation by applying principles that differ from the way they attracted the first generation. I also assumed a different set of principles apply when a small, established church grows into a large congregation as the surrounding neighborhood burgeons.

4. *Non-benchmark congregation.* Several mainline congregations attract continual national attention. Their innovative, well-publicized mission and ministry set a standard for others. Their ministers regularly tell their stories at conventions and workshops. I already knew what they do. I wanted to know about the highly effective congregation that gets little public notice.

17

Study results determined that the reality was more complex than assumed. Congregational vitality may or may not result from replacing traditional worship with a more contemporary style. Deciding to organize congregational life around small prayer groups may or may not invigorate the faith community's spiritual life. Renewal simply does not always follow a uniform, predictable pattern. I encountered congregations that have adopted what I call the "Evangelical Megachurch Model." If Willow Creek, the Community of Joy, or some other benchmark congregation suggests it, they try it. Often this brings great success. On the other hand, not all mainlines renew that way. Some remarkably vital tall-steeple churches adhere to very traditional ways.

I visited and/or conferred with some fifty congregations. They worshiped, programmed, nurtured, and organized for ministry and mission in a variety of ways. Their ministers varied widely in theological stance, leadership style, and personal demeanor. Some congregations fit the definition of the high-commitment church. Others make few demands on their members. Some think of themselves as mission posts on the frontier of a post-Christian world. Others operate on the assumption Christendom still flourishes and God calls them to form "Christian citizens for a Christian world."[2]

In looking past these differences, a discernable pattern of shared characteristics emerged. In spite of all the different ways of being and doing church, it became obvious that *renewal happens when intentional, high-expectation leadership works within the congregation's historical understanding—i.e., its story—to plan for and sustain a vital faith community where mission is clear and worship as well as program are indigenous to the life of the congregation.*

Although this study was limited to renewal in older, not necessarily household name, tall-steeple mainlines, some insights have application for established congregations of other sizes and circumstances. These common principles concern leadership, congregational ethos, and approaches to change. Specifically, I contend that renewal requires:

1. Leaders, both lay and clergy, who articulate clear visions, plan thoroughly, and set high expectations.

2. A faith community whose worship and program so vibrate with the presence of God that the structures of meaning for people are empowered.

3. A thorough understanding of the importance of the congregation's story. A good accounting of the way the church thinks about and talks about itself will not only describe the past and explain the way it organizes in the present, but also determine the way it plans for change.

Each chapter in this book explains one element of renewal. Each discussion is preceded by a brief description of a vital congregation that illustrates that principle. Chapter 1 contends that renewing congregations are places of spiritual vitality. Chapters 2 and 3 describe why a thorough knowledge of the congregation's sacred story—more technically, its subculture—is mandatory for both administration and change. Chapters 4 through 8 discuss characteristics I found common to every vibrant, renewing congregation: a vision, a plan, a mission focus, a demand for excellence, and a commitment to keep worship and program indigenous to the local congregation. Chapter 9 offers the longer perspective. Mainline congregations have been doing renewal for generations. The final chapter gives a word of hope. In spite of the rumors, the news about mainlines is better than expected.

WHERE ENGLISH IS SPOKEN WITHOUT A TRACE OF ACCENT

Saint Columba's Church of Scotland

London, England

A colleague shook his head in despair and said, "The European church should be placed on the endangered species list. Very few people ever darken the door of any church. We visited England last year and worshiped in an enormous cathedral. Sixteen people huddled in a corner of a sanctuary designed to seat two thousand. How sad! Christianity is in trouble in Europe."

How many times I have heard that lament. Imagine my delight at discovering a pocket of congregational vitality in an upscale London neighborhood. While on vacation, I visited Saint Columba's, one of two London congregations of the Church of Scotland. The place bustled with people and activity on an otherwise ordinary summer morning. The building, a large limestone structure, nestles in a residential area just a few blocks from the elegant Harrod's department store. The original nineteenth-century building was destroyed by German bombs in 1941 and not rebuilt until 1955. For more than a decade, the congregation worshiped in what remained of the basement.

On the Sunday I visited, nearly three hundred people comfortably filled the nave.[1] They ranged from young couples with infants in arms to the aged with canes. Saint Columba's congregants reflect London's age demography. The faith community's color differences also represent the city—mostly white, with a sprinkling of representatives from the British Empire from India to Africa. Youngsters abounded. Over thirty little ones were excused after a "children's sermon." In keeping with the American tradition, it was aimed over the kids' heads and directly at the adults. Following the worship service, a large contingent adjourned to the basement for an inexpensive lunch of quiche, salad, hard-boiled eggs, and tomatoes, with fresh strawberries and heavy cream for dessert.

Other than perhaps the two-dollar lunch, nothing easily explains why Saint Columba's flourishes when other London religious communities flounder. Neither the pastor nor his associate offers electrifying leadership. The church does not favor contemporary flair over traditional ways. Typical for the Church of Scotland, clergy wear robes and academic stoles. They lead the service from kneeling benches faced away from the congregation. The choir—a paid, double quartet—offers only classical anthems. The Sunday I attended the choir sang a vaguely familiar Mendelssohn and a totally unrecognized Elgar. The congregation sings from the standard "words only" Scottish hymnal. Although published in a recent generation, most hymns were written prior to the twentieth century. Of the six we sang, I knew only one tune. The congregation seemed equally unfamiliar.

Let me offer an explanation for why I could not be certain whether or not the congregation knew the hymns. I once served a congregation that had two male lay leaders who loved to sing. Unfortunately, both sang loudly but not very well. In fact, when the lay leaders sat near each other, their robust voices resonated like an oversized but off-key tuning fork. They drowned out the forty-two-rank pipe organ and confounded the singing efforts of the remainder of the congregation. For the good of this church, and by unanimous official board action, these leaders were charged never to sing near each other.

At Saint Columba's, I sat in front of an elderly woman of similar vocal ability who sang with even greater gusto. She loved the hymns. Unfortunately, congregants in at least a dozen surrounding pews could not hear the organ sufficiently to follow the tune.

The sermon for the morning focused on what it means to be part of the Church of Scotland. Using the prologue to the Church's Statement of Faith, the pastor offered a point-by-point, infrequently illustrated, exposition on the importance of the creeds and history of the Church of Scotland. While it was interesting, one could not characterize the homily as scintillating.

Throughout the worship hour, I pondered what kept Saint Columba's vital. It does not offer an upbeat, contemporary worship format. I doubt that the work of either Mendelssohn or Elgar provides the music for creating this oasis of Christian community in a desert of religious indifference. By the end of the morning, I began to understand. Saint Columba's is a Scottish church in London, England. Eighty percent of the congregation either comes from Scotland or has married a Scot. The members of color emigrated from the British Empire but grew up in Scottish Presbyterian churches in their home countries.

These congregants travel across metropolitan London to spend not only Sunday morning but much of the day with their own people. The names of members at Saint Columba's sound familiar. The coffee-fellowship conversations touch on common experiences. Saint Columba's reminds sojourners of home. To those who grew up in the Highlands around Loch Ness, or who long for the narrow streets in the oldest parts of Edinburgh, English is spoken at Saint Columba's without a trace of accent.

The appeal, however, is more than bagpipes, haggis, and kilts. Saint Columba's stands as an outpost reminder of home on the post-Christian frontier. The morning I attended, the Epistle lesson appropriately came from 1 Peter 2:10-12: "Once you were not a people, but now you are God's people . . . Beloved, I urge you as aliens and exiles . . . Conduct yourselves honorably among the Gentiles, so that . . . they may see your honorable deeds and glorify God" (NRSV).

The ministers and lay leaders in this faith community work hard at building community. They place a high priority on pastoral care and hospitality. Saint Columba's Church of Scotland intends to be familiar to those separated from family.

Saint Columba's showed no awareness of the American discussions about the trend toward informal worship, the need to replace the pipe organ with an electronic keyboard, the necessity of organizing the entire membership into small prayer/share groups, or any of the other things frequently advocated as "essential" to congregational renewal and vitalization. This congregation models the enclaved, Christ-centered, loving family.

There are congregations in the United States that stay vital by appealing to national, sectional, or racial heritage. Emphasizing ethnic specificity will not, however, renew most congregations. What works in the Chelsea neighborhood of London will not transfer *en masse* to the Colonies. On the other hand, the fundamental lessons must be noted. God's people long to be accepted and loved in the midst of a faith community. It empowers meaning in their lives. People come to church in hopes of encountering Ultimate Reality. Saint Columba's flourishes because that hope is realized.

Where People Encounter Ultimate Reality

The Church of the Resurrection, Leawood, Kansas, models how to start a mainline church. In its first eight years of existence, this United Methodist congregation has followed a traditional pattern for worship, mission, and ministry, and has grown from a committee to a Sunday morning attendance of well over four thousand. The church has an incredible location in the fastest-growing area of suburban Kansas City. The gifted senior minister, Adam Hamilton, knows and applies the church growth literature well. Church of the Resurrection has ample parking, a well-appointed nursery, an outstanding children's ministry, extensive small-group ministry, high visibility, good accessibility, outstanding music, and professional signage. The congregation does what every mainline church consultant recommends, and it flourishes.

A great location with plenty of parking does not, however, explain everything. Some faith communities languish in great locations with an abundance of parking. I also visited flourishing tall steeples in less than ideal locations with little parking. First United Methodist Church sits at the corner of Main and Perry near the downtown of Peoria, Illinois. Unlike in some cities, this downtown has not undergone a renaissance. A series of "down and dirty" strip joints and adult bookstores line the street across from First Church. A few years ago, the congregation mounted a zoning petition drive to limit the expansion of the pornography industry and keep it from totally encircling the church.

In 1915, when the present building was erected, many in

the congregation walked to church. Today, everyone drives. Still, nine hundred people per Sunday find their way to worship at this three-thousand-member, very traditional church. Many drive past at least a dozen other churches in far more appealing neighborhoods. Certainly the congregants do not come for the opportunity to view the advertisements in tavern windows or to see an inebriated customer sleeping it off in the alley across the street. Something happens at First Church that attracts a crowd.

First Plymouth Congregational Church, Lincoln, Nebraska, selected its site for proximity to the state capitol. With the changing times came changing traffic patterns. Those nine blocks to the capitol transformed into a labyrinth of confusion. Today, a newcomer to Lincoln needs a map and a compass to find what was once an ideal location. The church is buried on a side street. Its residential surroundings make accessibility difficult. The neighboring forest of trees and apartment buildings make visibility negligible. Still, First Plymouth Congregational remains a leading church in the city. Something about this faith community draws a crowd.

Even Preaching and Program Do Not Explain It

"What does it take to renew the witness and ministry of a mainline congregation?"

I asked that question everywhere I went. The answers differed according to the strength of the congregation and its leadership. James Moore, Saint Luke's United Methodist Church in Houston, Texas, regularly publishes his sermons. The day I was in his office, seven different volumes of his writings sat on a corner of his desk. He believes in and practices the centrality of the pulpit ministry. He is convinced that churches stay strong by the preaching of the Word.

Dick Wills, Christ United Methodist Church in Fort Lauderdale, Florida, whose congregation has a very extensive small-group ministry, says worship and being in a small group are co-equal in value and priority.

Second Presbyterian Church, Bloomington, Illinois, has a choir for every age group and circumstance. More than sixty years ago, the church started a children and youth choir program that involves nearly four hundred people each week. The summer youth program takes seventy-five teenagers on summer choir tour. The senior minister does not consider preaching his greatest skill. A small-group ministry has yet to emerge from the planning stages. Vocal music keeps the congregation strong.

Otis Young, Lincoln, Nebraska, attributes First Plymouth congregation's continuing strength in mission and ministry to a competent, long-tenured staff; outstanding educational program; and a well-done, traditional worship service that features sound preaching and classical music. The members also make certain the message gets out. They televise their worship services on several different cable stations throughout the state of Nebraska.

Hu Auburn, Bay Village, Ohio, pastors a Presbyterian congregation with a very strong small-group ministry as well as large music program. The church's music has a strong instrumental component. One of the worship services is led by a one-hundred-piece orchestra. This fits well with the contemporary worship style the congregation uses. The people do not respond as well to the traditional worship that works very well for other congregations.

Cecil Bliss, in Lincoln, Nebraska, leads a congregation that does not focus narrowly. Saint Mark's United Methodist Church has strong music programs, offers multiple small-group opportunities, does worship services in styles ranging from country western to rock and roll to traditional, and has a recreation program that involves nearly fifteen hundred people on one hundred forty different athletic teams.

"How do mainline tall-steeple churches renew for mission and ministry?" The answer cannot be found in a simple analysis of circumstances or behavior. Too many different styles of being and doing exist among them. That which cuts across all of them, however, is that tall steeples have a spiritual vitality for which building, parking, location, programs, and worship styles cannot fully account.

Places of Spiritual Synergy

Chromium plus nickel plus steel equals an alloy ten times stronger than any one component. Whatever happens when those metals combine into that alloy happens in the vital tall steeples. By careful planning and visioning, tall steeples do the right things. By setting high standards, they also do things right. The results, however, go beyond what might reasonably be expected from doing the right things in the right way. To paraphrase the mission statement of First Church of Christ, Wethersfield, Connecticut,[2] these congregations model a positive, affirming, need-fulfilling faith message that energizes and transforms human lives by the power of the Holy Spirit.

People may anticipate that preaching, music, and program will be outstanding, but they do not come to church to be entertained, to learn, or to hear an encouraging word. People come in hopes that a corner of the ordinariness of this world be lifted to offer them a glimpse of Ultimate Reality.

Passion for a Life of Faith

I stood with the crowd in the church lobby, waiting for the early service to conclude. I overheard a young couple speak excitedly with the husband's parents, who were visiting from out of town. This Generation X couple bubbled with enthusiasm about what brought them to the church. They spoke of a friendly congregation. The minister preached great sermons. The nursery provided outstanding child care. Every time they came to worship, they had a positive experience.

I heard similar discussions repeated numerous times in different churches in different locations. People seldom find the right words to wrap comfortably around their experience, but these congregations *en masse* exude a passion for life and faith that infect individual congregants. People sense that something meaningful happens on the faith journey they take in this community of believers. They get excited about it. The church leaders get excited about it.

John Cobb makes the point that in order for the mainlines to renew, they must reclaim an understanding of God's mystery, spirit, Wisdom, and justice.[3] This happens in the vital tall steeples I studied. Their leaders spoke confidently and passionately of a personal faith strong on mystery, spirit, Wisdom, and justice. Few seemed to have the usual mainline reticence about calling for passion, commitment, responsibility, and accountability from their congregations.

When Mystery Touches the Pastor's Life

Although far from a majority, several of these senior ministers spoke of religious experiences that might be characterized as mysterious, if not mystical. One pastor told of waking in the middle of the night with a message ringing in his ears: "Go for the long haul and go deep!" This he understood as encouragement to endure on the present path toward renewal and to challenge the people to a more substantive theological understanding of their mission and ministry.

Another minister told of a spiritual conversion experience following a time of significant crises in the congregation. The congregation's key lay leader was murdered and his son wounded in a robbery. This came on the heels of a tragedy in the minister's family. The sting of grief had yet to lessen when the minister, in the quiet of a summer's visit to the family summer home, heard the distinct sound of a trumpet playing "How Great Thou Art." A sense of God's healing love flooded over him. Since that experience, he says that he preaches God's love with greater conviction. "God worked in my life, and my preaching bears witness to it."

Several ministers reported the regular practice of personal spiritual disciplines and solitary retreats. These proved a way to discern God's leading for themselves and the congregation.

When asked "Where in the life of this church do people experience the presence of God?" most ministers spoke of the importance of small groups; of the adult Sunday school classes that, once in place, can last a half century; of hands-on mission projects, such as soup kitchens and Habitat for Humanity houses that permit people to be instruments of God's love to others; and of worship services where the music calls the angels to hover near.

No minister ever said, "I have encountered God's presence in my life; others can see the reflection on my face." In fact, I do not remember any layperson saying, "I can catch a glimpse of God in the life of the pastor."

No one said that. However, I suspect many could.

YOUR PREDECESSOR IS NOT YOUR ENEMY

St. Luke's United Methodist Church

Indianapolis, Indiana

A handful of people joined together in 1953 to create a new faith community on the northern growing edge of Indianapolis. As stated in current publicity, "they had no way of knowing that the church they were starting would become the Midwest's largest United Methodist congregation."[1]

The church is located one block from Meridian, Indianapolis's main north-south street, on West 86th Street, the city's most heavily traveled shopping district. When I visited, plumbers, brick masons, and carpenters swarmed the facility. They were applying their skills to bring a very large new sanctuary and expanded education building out of land that a generation ago grew corn and soybeans. The architecture of the new building continued the distinctive design of the old.

The senior minister, Kent Millard, began our conversation by telling the church's story. A group of committed laypeople from a central city congregation had a vision. They persisted despite a less-than-enthusiastic district superintendent. The faith community grew steadily but unspectacularly until 1968, when Carver McGriff was appointed pastor. In McGriff's twenty-six-year ministry, St. Luke's grew from nine hundred to four thousand members.

Millard waxed eloquent about how his predecessor built the congregation around his "clever, thoughtful, self-deprecating" preaching. "People came to this church to hear McGriff preach," he explained. In addition, McGriff had the gift for bringing together strong staff to develop sound programs that responded to people's needs. Twenty-six years ago this policy of setting staff free to do ministry resulted in "a singles ministry that still draws three hundred people on a Wednesday night." Millard insisted, "We have one of the best singles ministries in the country."

Our conversation continued as Millard described how he began his ministry at St. Luke's by listening carefully to the congregation. He quickly realized that his predecessor keyed this faith community's understanding of themselves. Their love of Carver McGriff made them into a congregation that expect great preaching. Millard never thought of preaching as his greatest gift, but he made the sermon a higher ministerial priority. His preaching, he claims, has benefited.

Many pastors dread the thought of following a twenty-six-year ministry. They know that changing the way the congregation does ministry will be difficult. When the people's love for the predecessor continues unabated, the next minister fears his or her tenure has only three possibilities: short, painful, or short and painful.

The previous senior minister can be seen as a problem to solve. Millard resolved to think of McGriff as an asset on which to build. Rather than ignore the former senior minister, he sought McGriff's perspective. McGriff, after all, had been an integral part of this faith community for a quarter century and had much to offer. The two men regularly meet over breakfast to discuss their mutual agenda of keeping St. Luke's strong. Millard thinks of McGriff as his mentor, not his enemy. Their deepening friendship makes it possible for Millard to say to the church, "Carver and I want the same things for St. Luke's. We will continue our mission as 'an open community of Christians gathering to seek, celebrate, live, and share the love of God for all creation.' "

From the congregation's perspective, leadership made a seamless transition from McGriff to Millard. Whereas worship attendance frequently drops after a long pastorate, in Millard's first year it increased by one hundred and fifty each Sunday. That growth continues. Worship and education space have been maximized. The congregation responded to the overcrowding by underwriting the $13 million capital campaign that funds the new education wing and fifteen-hundred-seat sanctuary.

In addition to the emphasis on worship, Millard has continued McGriff's policy of setting staff and laity free to develop strong programs that respond to people's needs. Consequently, the innovative quality of the mission and ministry of St. Luke's continues to escalate.

Obviously, St. Luke's United Methodist Church benefits from the special relationship between Carver McGriff and Kent Millard. One should not, however, discount the strategy for transition that Millard developed. He began his ministry by listening to the people. He wanted to learn their story. He quickly discovered that McGriff occupied the hero role in their saga. Rather than rail against it, wisdom dictated the new senior minister find a way to make the best of it. As the adage holds, "It is always easier to steer the wagon in the direction it's being pulled." Millard did that. He consulted McGriff, earned his respect and support, then assured the congregation the two agreed on where they were headed. Millard continued using major constructs in the congregation's story put in place by Carver McGriff. The mission continued. The program grew in directions it was already headed. Laity and staff continue to be encouraged to offer their best. Worship remains central to their way of being church. Preaching dwells at the heart of the worship. The new sanctuary even continues the distinctive architecture.

Keeping the same story does not preclude making changes. St. Luke's has undergone significant changes. However, those changes come within the overall story the congregation tells about how it understands itself.

Pay Heed to the Story

According to a Hasidic story, founding Rabbi Israel Shem Tov always meditated at a certain place in the forest. When misfortune threatened the Jews, he went there to light a fire and say a special prayer. A miracle, so the story goes, always occurred when he did this, and the misfortune was averted.

During the leadership tenure of Maggid of Mezritch, a disciple of Israel Shem Tov, the Jewish people were threatened again. Maggid followed the example of his mentor. He went to the same place in the forest and prayed: "Master of the Universe, listen! I do not know how to light the fire, but I am able to say the prayer." Again, a miracle occurred. The Jewish people were rescued from disaster.

With the third generation came another threat. Hasidic leader Rabbi Moshe-leib of Sasov went into the forest to pray: "I do not know how to light the fire. I do not know the special prayer. I do, however, know this sacred place, and this must be sufficient." Indeed, it was sufficient. Another miracle occurred.

In still a later generation, it fell to Rabbi Israel of Rizhin to lead the people through a crisis. He sat at home in his armchair and prayed, "I do not know the words to the special prayer. I do not know how to light the fire. I do not even know the location of the sacred place in the woods. All I know is the story about the fire, the prayer, the special place in the woods. I can only tell that story, and this must be sufficient."

The French version concludes: "And it was sufficient. For God made man because he loves stories."[2]

One cannot help but note the final sentence's double

meaning. The "he" might refer to God or humankind. Either understanding makes sense. People come to know God through stories. Stories shape self-identity for people. Both God and people love to communicate with stories.

The Story Constitutes the Most Important Factor in Renewal

My study was limited to established, large, mainline congregations. I assumed these would differ from new, small, and/or evangelical ones. After visiting more than thirty tall-steeple churches, having extensive phone conversations with another half dozen, and gathering printed information on another dozen, even more differences became obvious. Congregational differences go well beyond the constructs of age, size, and denominational affiliation. Every congregation differs from every other congregation. Grouping by size, demographics, denomination, economics, sociology, theology, or any other set of categories may be handy but falls short of a comprehensive explanation for a church's way of thinking and doing.

To understand a congregation one must learn its story. How does it understand itself? How does it integrate its history into both present understanding and plans for the future? How does it talk about the gospel? In renewing faith communities, leadership knows to deal with the congregation's story. In my study of large, established, mainline tall steeples nothing proved a greater constant.

Every faith community has a distinct, thick, meaning-laden way to express its faith and religious behavior. Research shows the story, more technically called the congregational subculture, to be as unique and rich as those of the religious communities studied by any cultural anthropologist or foreign missionary.[3]

A congregation's story, the narrative self-understanding and way to explain how and why it does mission and ministry, gathers around everything from the collective spiritual journeys of the membership to the styles of leadership offered by past and present ministers to the events in the community's history to the ways it interprets meaning and empowers the experiences of members, leaders, and events. The story also will both shape and be shaped by everything from architecture to neighborhood location.

Wise leadership knows to pay close attention to the faith community's collective narrative. As David Fisher, the pastor of the Colonial Church in Edina, Minnesota, put it: "Around here the congregation's story is almost as important as the gospel."

History and Tradition Shape the Story

Some congregations remember significant people or events in their narratives. William Major, founding pastor of First Christian Church, Bloomington, owned the assembly hall where his good friend Abraham Lincoln helped establish the Illinois Republican Party.

The Allen brothers, early settlers of Houston, gave the land for First United Methodist Church.

Second Presbyterian Church, Indianapolis, still displays the pulpit chair used by Henry Ward Beecher when he pastored the congregation in the 1830s.

First Church of Christ, Wethersfield, Connecticut, dates from 1635. The members worship in a meeting house dedicated in 1761. Jonathan Edwards, key figure in the Great Awakening, probably attended the church while a college student. Timothy Dwight, Jonathan Edwards's grandson and leader in the Second Great Awakening, worshiped in the present meeting house during the Revolutionary War

37

and may have had this faith community in mind when he wrote, "I love thy church, O Lord."[4]

These congregations each have a significant history that influences present understandings. The past cannot be changed. The congregations can only decide how to incorporate it into their present and future stories. History can be either a millstone holding them down or a springboard propelling them into the future.

The Wethersfield, Connecticut, congregation meets in a facility erected more than two hundred years ago. The congregation must constantly deal with that. A visitor sharpened the issue by stopping the minister on the street to ask, "Tell me, sir, is that a church or is it a museum?" The congregation can tell its story in ways that makes either a possibility. Wethersfield has chosen to connect positively to its history. Former minister Donald Morgan claimed, "Two of the greatest figures of the greatest awakenings America has ever known were closely identified with First Church of Christ in Wethersfield. We are thrilled to believe our current renewal and vitality are faithful reflections of the rich faith heritage of New England."[5]

Even though the Colonial Church of Edina does not have the long history of the Wethersfield congregation, it takes New England tradition just as seriously. The architecture of the building in suburban Minneapolis was inspired by a Cape Cod meeting house built in 1717. The congregants call their campus "the Village" and honor Congregational church history by naming the Jonathan Edwards Youth Room and the Abigail Adams Kitchen. In the foyer of this nearly new building stands a clear fiberglass case with a tiny, unremarkable chunk of old wood. The plaque proudly claims the wood came from the English ship *The Mayflower*, which landed at Plymouth, Massachusetts, in 1620.

The fact that First Church of Christ in Wethersfield was actually constructed more than two centuries ago and the

Colonial Church in Edina only reflects architecture of that era makes little difference. American history shapes the self-understanding of both congregations. When asked to describe their faith community, each tells a story that connects them to early New England Congregationalism.

Important Traditions from Ordinary Events

Congregations do not need Wethersfield's long history or Edina's valuing of the seventeenth and eighteenth centuries to develop deep convictions about their stories. Every congregation does this. Each faith community has its own unique self-identity and its own way to do mission and ministry. Its own language for expressing the faith. In his in-depth study of two North Georgia congregations, James Hopewell concluded that a group of people cannot gather for what they feel to be religious purposes without developing their own subculture.[6]

Even the inexperienced ecclesiologist recognizes underlying story differences in the advertisements on Saturday's newspaper religion page. The congregation that claims to be "The Friendly Church in the Heart of Elmwood" probably has a different self-understanding than the faith community that regales in its theological specificity: "A Pre-millennial, Spirit-led, Full Gospel, Bible-believing Church Which Condemns Sin While Loving Most Sinners." The claim "The City's Oldest Congregation" says something different about the faith community's understanding of history than the congregation that advertises itself as "Still Worshiping from the 1836 Muldorfian Language Prayer Book." "The City's Most Exciting Church" probably understands mission differently than "An Open and Affirming Church Dedicated to Justice."

Rather than requiring significant historical persons or

events, the congregation's story emerges from the events in the lives of ordinary people gathering as a faith community. A congregation's story both shapes and is shaped by the way the congregants worship, the neighborhood in which they are located, the character of their architecture, the leadership styles and personalities of their ministers and laity, as well as a multitude of other factors.

The congregation begins assembling its story before closing the membership charter. Out of collective experience, the founders decide on core values, determine mission, set vision, establish patterns for doing ministry, and find their own special way to express the faith. Depending on the story theme, the congregation becomes large or stays small by welcoming many or just a few into its community.

Denominations help produce congregations similar to one another. They cannot, however, force them all through the same cookie cutter. Each faith community makes distinctive contributions to its own story. At times, denominational officials do not even recognize a faith community as one of their own children.

A few years after the chartering, the basic themes of the congregation's story slide into place. The congregation then uses its story to communicate with itself, to express love and faith, to govern, and to decide how to make changes in its corporate behavior.[7] It also uses the story to attract others. Visitors join or continue their search based on whether or not the congregation's subculture resonates to the story of their personal faith journeys. Even when they do not articulate a theological reason for it, people join a certain faith community because they find agreement with the way that particular branch of the family of God does worship, study, mission, and ministry.

As time passes, a congregation's story grows richer and more meaning-laden. The second, third, and fourth generations hear the story, join the community, add new details, modify older understandings, and extinguish elements they find inappropriate. The story spreads through congregational life like kudzu wrapped through a chain-link fence. It permeates everything.

The Story Becomes More Than Congregational Thinking and Doing

By its story a congregation states its beliefs, describes the way it goes about its mission, and even determines the pattern for everyday administrative transactions. James Hopewell insisted that even more significantly, the story accounts for God's intention for the faith community. Through its narrative self-understanding, the congregation perceives divine leading in the "worldwide mission for establishing God's shalom."[8]

No wonder congregations resist changing their ways of thinking and doing. They not only believe God had a hand in writing their stories, but also believe God uses their stories as channels for service. What may seem trivial to an outsider is, to the people in the faith community, sacred story. "The legend of God's plan, if only its sounds and signs can be heard and read."[9]

Elements of Story Can Become Overly Sacred

Unfortunately, details about how God calls a people into being and leads them into ministry can slide to the center of congregational life and become an object for adoration. An East Coast pastor discovered that his unorthodox, even heretical, sermons never get a negative response. A few years ago, the church received over a million dollars from the sale of property. Without a single complaint, the mem-

41

bers set aside the proceeds for a ministry to meet human needs in their city. However, when the minister suggested moving the pulpit a few feet to the left and the lectern a couple feet to the right, the faith community nearly exploded in protest.[10] For some reason, the unchangeable elements in the congregation's story were stretched to conclude that God determined pulpit furniture location.

Forty years ago, a congregation grew out of a neighborhood Bible study. The highly committed people in that group covenanted to support the church financially. In faith, they agreed to invite others to join them, but never to ask for money. Giving, they decided, must be a faithful response. As a sign of that commitment, they agreed not to "pass the plate" at the Bible study. When their study group grew into a worshiping community, they continued the practice of not receiving an offering. Four decades later, the congregation has institutionalized the Bible study practice. They never ask for money and never pass an offering tray during worship. This congregation now averages more than six hundred in worship. When searching for a new senior minister, the terms of call include the commitment never to have an offering tray passed in worship. What started as a sign of the faith commitment of the founding few has become the sacred practice of a large community.

The Storyteller Must Know the Story

Long pastorates characterize vital tall-steeple congregations. Tenures of twenty or thirty years are common. Changes do, of course, still happen. When they do, the best transitions occur when the new minister listens carefully for the congregation's story, then speaks to the people in the language and thought forms to which they are accustomed.

Dallas's Mark Craig is described as "very respectful of the tradition." From the day he was appointed, "he held up the history of Highland Park United Methodist Church as the standard for the present and future." According to a colleague on staff, Craig continues to build on the congregation's understanding of itself as a leader in mission. This includes advocating justice, as the church did in the 1960s when it played a leadership role in local civil rights issues.

Richard Wing says he learned very quickly that the members of First Community Church, Columbus, Ohio, call themselves the "Church That Plows a Wider Path." They think of themselves as open to many different people and many different ways of thinking. Wing decided early that his ministry would do best in Columbus if he continued to talk about the church that travels the wider path.

Effective leaders get to know the story and keep it before the congregation. It can probably be said of every established congregation, "Around here the story is almost as important as the gospel."

THE ART OF MOVING A
CONGREGATION INTO A NEW ERA

First Community Church
Columbus, Ohio

First Community Church serves from two locations. The congregation calls them the North and South Campus. The older, South Campus occupies most of a city block in an upscale residential neighborhood near the Ohio State University and downtown Columbus. The homes along Cambridge Boulevard, the six-lane parkway on which the Ohio limestone building is located, probably appear regularly in the Columbus equivalent of *House Beautiful* magazine. Jack Nicklaus learned to play golf at the nearby Scioto Country Club. The evening I arrived at the South Campus, Dave Thomas, the CEO of Wendy's, attended a wedding. His daughter after whom the restaurant chain is named was married at the church several years ago.

Despite the grand building and neighborhood, the South Campus has all the shortcomings expected in an older residential location: low visibility, difficult accessibility, and a significant shortage of parking. These problems are not new. In the 1950s, a beloved senior minister began to talk about the need to relocate the church. Toward that end, the congregation purchased twenty acres, only to sell the property twenty years later during a time of financial difficulty.

Leadership never gave up trying to solve the problems presented by the less-than-ideal location. Several years ago, the congregation purchased acreage for the North Campus in a growing area of the city about five miles from Cambridge Boulevard. The leadership intended to build a new facility and relocate. Toward that end, an architect presented plans for a building that resembled the limestone Cambridge Boulevard facility.

A significant difference of opinion divided the congregation. Conflict, however, is no stranger to First Community. Barry Johnson, the senior minister at that time, commented that the congregation's history of being "intentionally diverse, inclusive and, as an institution, willing to put up with almost all forms of behavior" lent itself to a state of perpetual conflict.[1]

When the vote failed, the leaders rethought the issue. They abandoned relocation plans, reframed the issue, and presented the new site as "The Center for Extended Ministry." The plan called for the Cambridge Boulevard location to be maintained and for the church to begin doing ministry in two locations.

With the expected amount of controversy, conflict, and difficulty, the proposal was accepted and funded. At the new ministry site, the church erected Sunday school classes and a fellowship hall to serve as temporary worship space. The church plans eventually to expand the Center for Extended Ministry with more education space and a large, permanent sanctuary.

Even though First Community Church operates effectively as "one church in two locations," each site has its own identity and is developing its own approach to mission and ministry. The North Campus has the "feel" of a suburban congregation. It specializes in youth ministry and offers informal as well as contemporary worship opportunities. The South Campus maintains a more formal, traditional worship and program in an established neighborhood. The television ministry, which can reach two million people in Greater Columbus, originates at the South Campus. Each location ministers to a slightly different segment of the Columbus population. Both locations, however, continue the ministry of excellence for which First Community is known.

Keeping two locations up and moving requires significant energy and coordination. Each Sunday morning, Richard Wing, the senior minister, leads worship at both campuses. At 8:30 A.M., about forty people begin First Community Church's worship experience with a prayer and communion service in the chapel of the South Campus. Then the activity moves to the new North Campus. At 9:00, they hold an informal but traditional worship service and children's Sunday school. This is followed by a 10:15 contemporary service. The sermon comes early in this "guitar-led," upbeat forty-five-minute praise service. As soon as the homily ends, the minister heads for the South Campus and the formal, traditional 11:00 worship on Cambridge Boulevard. Meanwhile, at the North Campus, several hundred adults and youth attend another Christian education session.

The faith community responds well. On the late spring morning I attended, congregants comfortably filled every service at both locations. I was informed that participation has grown nearly 40 percent since opening the North Campus. Wing explained how they made the change. "*Transition* is an important word for this congregation. We are always transitioning to something." He went on to speak of the pain surrounding buying and selling property; progressing through a series of senior ministers; disappointment and struggles over relocating; the decision to be one church at two locations; and the eventual fulfillment of that plan.

46

Wing credits the transition to the congregation's present effectiveness to persistence, strong lay leadership, and a tradition of shrugging off failure and disappointment. "God must really love this congregation," he said.

It also helps that First Community Church does ministry in a way that continues to attract people from across Columbus. The church has long been admired for its outstanding music and tradition of sound preaching. It has maintained the philosophy of pastoral care from "cradle to grave" since the 1950s and operates a youth program that continues to send twelve hundred kids to camp each summer. In addition, First Community proudly claims an early-childhood religious education program that ranks as one of the best in the city.

To all outward appearances, First Community differs radically from the church it was a couple of decades ago. However, close examination reveals that this faith community has merely become the next generation of what it has always been. The congregants' strengths have not changed. They continue their sacred story as a leading, innovative, liberal, mainline faith community known for great worship, education, mission, and youth ministry in an atmosphere of tolerance that encourages each person to continue his or her spiritual search. The present simply writes the next chapter in the congregation's story. This new chapter continues ministry as the congregants have always done it, but in a way appropriate to present circumstances as "one church in two locations."

Principles of Change in the Long-Established Church

Time has not been kind to Jim. In his prime, he stood six feet, six inches. Today, the crook in his back makes him closer to six feet. In his youth many judged him handsome. Now in his ninth decade, gravity tugs at his face transforming a once chiseled jaw into sagging jowls.

Jim's daughter, Sue, bears little resemblance to her father. He is enormous and has a commanding presence. She is quiet, petite, and refined. In spite of those physical and gender differences, careful observers seldom miss that Jim and Sue are related. They smile in a way that reveals their kinship. They nod their heads in the same peculiar way. They throw their left feet at the same angle when they walk. They also share characteristics that transcend physical appearance. Both love Christ's church and provide positive leadership to it. To know Sue is to experience the next generation of Jim.

Long-established congregations usually move through time in much the same way a family works its way through generations. Even though today never replicates yesterday, careful observation reveals linkages. In his tome on how the Soviet Union collapsed, former American Ambassador Jack Matlock goes beyond genetics to claim this principle for the social sciences as well: "People change. Societies change. But never totally. Features of the past never disappear, either from individuals or from society."[2]

This also describes congregational life. To paraphrase Matlock, society changes. Churches change. But never totally. Some features of a congregation's past never disappear. In a faith community's present, keen eyes detect remnants of what used to be.

Know This! Past, Present, and Future Always Differ

The world in which Christ's church does ministry changes constantly. Only a quarter of a century ago the annual starting salary of a teacher in the United States barely topped $8,000. The median sales price of a new home had yet to reach $40,000. A dime delivered a first-class letter.

Change, however, affects more than costs. We live differently today. People expect more space and more choices. New homes have more square footage than older homes. The mall, with its one hundred stores, has replaced the downtown department store. Twenty-seven different kinds of salsa now supplement ketchup. People simply demand more of everything. For instance, today's minister considers a desktop computer a tool of the trade, usually has e-mail, and plans for a cell phone with two incoming lines. The times make technology integral to pastoral ministry.

People expected less two decades ago. Only one company offered telephone service. Most television sets received only three network stations. New movies were shown only in theaters. A traveler paid the standard plane fare dictated by a government agency. Rather than expect technology, people seldom imagined it. The rare minister who thought a desktop computer possible was considered a comic, not a visionary.

The first few decades of the new century will continue significant social change. A simple projection of current trends leads us to expect the future will be a time of widespread disconnectedness resulting from the continued devaluing of neighborhood. The overvaluing of individualism will further erode a consensual social ethic. Unless resolved, present political realities will drive more and more capable people out of leadership. Unless punctuated by significant renewal and transformation, mainline churches can expect to draw an even smaller percentage of the total population.

Obviously, the long-established congregation must make changes appropriate to the times. We simply cannot move with vitality into a new century by doing the same things the same way. People of faith, of course, have always been faced with the need to change. Rumor has it that when ordered out of paradise, Adam remarked to Eve, "My dear, we live in an age of transition." Unfortunately, its constancy does not make change easy. We still struggle to find effective ways for the established congregation to renew itself into a different time.

Change: Two Species, Each with Two Subspecies

Theorists ordinarily put change into two distinct categories, first and second order.[3] Simple, operational, incremental course corrections constitute first-order change. Having the pipe organ tuned illustrates first-order change. Second order, frequently called a paradigm shift, involves metachange. Abandoning the use of the pipe organ in favor of drums, guitar, and keyboard illustrates a second-order change in the experience of worship. Generally, second order gets greater results than first-order change. It also produces higher levels of stress and requires more intentional management.

First- and second-order change can each be further divided into reactive and proactive. Anticipation of need distinguishes the two. Adjusting the heat in the sanctuary because twenty people complained illustrates first-order reactive change. Proactive first-order change anticipates a simple need and prepares for it. This happens, for instance, when an administrative staff person orders extra bulletins for Easter Sunday. The still vital faith community that relocates to the suburbs from a bustling downtown location undertakes a proactive second-order change. Reactive second-order change occurs when the congregation waits to relocate until the neighborhood is abandoned and the average age of the dozen remaining members approaches eighty.

Biology teaches that plants and animals differentiate by species. Reproductive isolation defines membership. A horse and zebra may look similar but do not produce viable offspring. A herd of zebras never "becomes" a herd of horses. By definition, horses and zebras hold membership in different species.

Common wisdom maintains that the differences between first and second order make them distinct species of change. First order does not "lead" to second order. Simple changes do not necessarily accumulate into paradigm shifts. While both are categories of change, they differ as significantly as the horse and zebra.

When I began my study, I assumed that principles of congregational renewal should be framed in terms of first- and second-order change being different species. In Kansas City, our congregation has been renewing by first-order change. We function on a model for mission and ministry that differs little from the mainlines of the past. All our changes have been proactive and reactive, first order. While results have been encouraging, I wonder, "Are we doing enough? Will fine-tuning our traditional Sunday morning be sufficient? Will we have to make a paradigm shift to a contemporary style of worship? In order to flourish into the next century, must we become something other than a traditional mainline congregation?"

51

The Story Must Be Considered When Planning for Change

I discovered that, while technically accurate, framing the issues solely in terms of first- and second-order change was not helpful. Older tall-steeple churches do not readily make paradigmatic shifts in mission and ministry simply because the external environment dictates the need.

Established congregations assess circumstances in the surrounding culture. They understand the need to change in accordance. They also pay close attention to their deeply embedded sacred stories. The church simply cannot undertake effective change without considering how the change affects its story.

A congregation uses its story in much the same way a computer uses an operating system. The story provides the constructs by which the congregation functions. The story—the subculture—offers the thought forms to structure the congregation's beliefs, the language to describe the way it goes about its mission, and the processes by which it patterns everyday administrative transactions. Any alteration the established congregation makes in anything, from the way it talks about issues of faith to where it locates the pulpit on the chancel, affects the way it thinks and talks about itself.

Consequently, a smooth and effective transition into a different environment must account for the role played by the story. This means doing more than ascertaining whether the situation dictates a first- or second-order change and applying an appropriate change strategy. It requires showing the faith community how that desired change relates to what the people believe about how God calls them to do mission and ministry.

Congregational Renewal Requires a New Chapter in the Story

Alfred North Whitehead once commented that "the art of progress is to preserve order amid change and to preserve change amid order."[4] An established congregation follows this advice by first assessing present circumstances and projecting future needs. Leadership then determines which aspects of the congregation's present story will serve well in the future, and which parts of the story need to be left behind. The fragments deemed helpful form the basis for writing the next chapter in the congregation's story. The faith community leaves behind unnecessary or inappropriate story lines, usually by neglecting to talk about them rather than confronting them. To the selections from the present story, the leadership may add compatible new elements, deemed beneficial for the move from present to future, and form what the congregation recognizes as the next chapter in its story. Leadership uses this newly revised story as the congregation's operating system by keeping it continually before the people. When this new chapter functions effectively, it pulls the faith community forward and renews it for mission and ministry.

When Kent Millard was first appointed to replace the retiring senior minister at St. Luke's United Methodist Church, he listened to how the people talked about themselves. He quickly learned that for more than a quarter of a century, St. Luke's considered worship central to its common life, and preaching central to worship. Administratively, St. Luke's functioned primarily as a "Sunday morning church." The congregants believed the former senior minister was the catalyst that held the congregation together. They also prided themselves on their capacity to set people free to do their own ministry.

The new senior minister wisely decided that the Millard chapter in St. Luke's history would be written by revising and updating these themes others had put in place. Consequently, most of the present congregation's ways of thinking and doing can be recognized as the next generation of what the church has always been. The move from Sunday-morning to seven-day-a-week church does represent a substantial new element in the congregation's story. In fact, it must be judged as nothing less than second-order change. However, since it mingles so thoroughly with the more familiar, it was accomplished without the usual trauma of a paradigmatic shift in congregational operations.

First Community Church in Columbus also continues the basic themes of its traditional story. The members of the congregation still think of themselves as a leading, innovative, liberal, mainline faith community known for great worship, education, mission, and youth ministry in an atmosphere of tolerance that encourages each person to continue his or her spiritual search. They simply have written a new chapter to guide them in a new day. This next generation of what they have always been includes doing ministry as "one church in two locations."

All Change Is Painful

Almost without exception, the tall-steeple congregations I studied renewed themselves by making incremental changes that maintained continuity with their past. While considerably less disruptive than trying to revitalize by making radical changes that ignore the congregation's historic ways of thinking and doing, one should not assume that this approach is stress-free. During the tenure of the previous minister, one congregation used a short responsive reading as a call to prayer in every worship service.

When the new minister arrived, the lay leadership told him to make a change. Those responsive readings, they said, were monotonous, lacked imagination, and added little to worship.

The new minister dropped the litany and added a sung chorus before the morning prayer. The change was first order. It did nothing to alter significantly the worship style. Most people appreciated the change. For the next several weeks, however, many, including several lay leaders who suggested it, commented on how much they missed the responsive reading. Those litanies may not have been particularly meaningful, but they were familiar. Losing them broke something loose deep in the psyche of the people.

Even a small, agreed upon, first-order modification will elicit discomfort. As Anatole France noted, "All changes, even the most longed for, have their melancholy. What we leave behind us is part of ourselves."[5] Every change hurts because it involves the loss of the familiar.

Change agents must always be alert to this reality. Discomfort comes even with changes intended to do nothing more than take the church into the next generation of what has always been. Carefully monitor accumulating discomfort. Learn the limits of what the leadership and the congregation can tolerate. Know when to push for more as well as when to back off and permit some healing to take place.

Expect Hard Work and Plan for the Long-term

The experienced tourist has learned that while overseas travel usually requires only half as many clothes as expected, one had best take twice as much film and three times as much money. The experienced church leader has learned that while renewing an established congregation may take only half as many radical changes as projected, it will take twice as long as anticipated and be three times more difficult than ever imagined. One can never overestimate the time and energy required.

A Disciples of Christ congregation felt the need to evaluate the format of its worship service. The congregation began the process by appointing a Worship and Liturgy Team. Led by the minister of music, it consisted of a cross-section of the membership. The team was charged to study the field of worship and relate emerging trends to the congregation's practices. They spent months reading the latest texts on renewing worship in mainline Protestantism, and reviewing seventy-five years of their worship bulletins. This study offered two significant insights: (1) the congregation could harmonize its traditional worship experience with the latest trends in the field by making only minor alterations; and (2) there had been no significant change in the order of worship in thirty years.

With facts in hand, the Worship and Liturgy Team decided to test the congregation's willingness to change. They drafted a survey that asked specific questions regarding individual preferences on a variety of worship-related topics. The survey was distributed in Sunday bulletins for one month. More than seven hundred surveys were returned and tabulated. Although a clear majority of the membership was willing to change, responders frequently limited that support to "nothing too extreme" and "not on regular basis."

The Worship and Liturgy Team deliberated for eighteen months before recommending that the Board of Elders approve a five-month period of "innovation in morning worship." As the governing body responsible for the spiritual health of the congregation, the elders debated and discussed the proposal thoroughly before adopting it.

The team developed a long list of simple, first-order

changes that might enhance the worship experience. These included: sing more contemporary hymns, even an occasional praise chorus; move the Lord's Prayer from after the Pastoral Prayer to after the Call to Worship; add a children's sermon at 11:00 A.M.; present the Scripture in various ways—through dramatic oral interpretation, a skit, congregational responsive reading, and singing a psalm; make less formal the procedures by which deacons and elders serve the Lord's Supper; and place the Lord's Supper after the sermon instead of preceding it.

The team felt the worship experience needed to be less rigid, to radiate more energy, and to be more participatory. Toward that end, liturgists worked to "be brief," "be ready," "be excited about what you do." Greeters and ushers were instructed on ways to make congregants feel welcomed. The entire worship experience was fine-tuned to make it less a spectator event and more an opportunity for participation.

A carefully selected, ongoing focus group met monthly to discuss their thoughts and feelings about the innovations. To ensure every constituency's input, twenty-seven other open-invitation meetings were held in various places and at different times. During the five months of experimentation, the Worship and Liturgy Team met at least biweekly to receive detailed written reports on feedback from the congregation, offer their own evaluations, and make alterations. At the end of the trial period, another survey was distributed and more than seven hundred responses were tabulated.

Based on all the information gathered, the Worship and Liturgy Team recommended to the elders that the innovations of the type and style experienced by the congregation in the past five months be continued on a permanent basis. This recommendation, accompanied by a fifteen-page report, was mailed to all eighty-five elders.

Even though, in the scheme of things, the innovations were minuscule and first order, a group of older elders were distressed enough to circulate a petition calling for a return to the format that had gone unchanged for three decades. After two more months of study by the elders, and a rancorous two-hour debate, 80 percent of the elders agreed to the resolution. It had taken three years to introduce nothing more than the next generation of traditional worship. Slight as the changes might be, however, the process set the church free to continue writing the next chapter of the congregation's story.

Leadership as Vision Casting and Storytelling

Obviously, the role of leadership as "vision casting" and as "tender of the sacred story" interfaces at "writing a new chapter." By definition, vision brings focus to a realistic, credible, attractive destination at which the congregation can aim. A well-written new chapter in their sacred story helps the people understand that this chosen route to the future maintains continuity with how God has dealt with their faith community throughout its history.

To bring vision and story together in a new chapter requires both competent and creative leadership. Malignant themes from the past can be extinguished. The vision must be possible. The congregation must resonate with the new chapter. A vital future depends on bringing these together.

DISCIPLES OF CHRIST WITH VISION IN THE NATION'S CAPITAL

National City Christian Church
Washington, D.C.

The National City Christian Church in Washington, D.C., refers to itself as the "National Cathedral of the Disciples of Christ." This magnificent structure, designed by the architect of the Jefferson Memorial, is located on Thomas Circle, just a few blocks from the White House. It has one of the largest pipe organs in Washington. An ornate white marble pulpit and large baptistry dominate the sanctuary chancel.

Stained-glass windows honor two presidents from the Christian Church (Disciples of Christ) associated with this faith community. James A. Garfield is the only ordained minister to serve as president of the United States. Lyndon Johnson was an active member and regular attender. Both the inauguration prayer service and funeral for President Johnson took place in this sanctuary. This congregation has a rich history.

From its beginning, this sacred place has served as a "Disciple home away from home." The resident membership has never been extremely large but has always been welcoming to Disciple visitors, elected officials, and those having business with the federal government. This ministry of hospitality dwells at the center of the congregation's story.

Times and circumstances change. For decades numbers have been declining. The church can no longer rely on prominent politicians and tourists from Disciple congregations. Notable politicians with Disciples of Christ heritages are in short supply. A declining denomination sends fewer and fewer visitors to the city. The area around Thomas Circle is predominantly Hispanic and African American. Most resident members drive from distant neighborhoods and outlying suburbs. Significant efforts were made to reach out to the people surrounding the church, but with limited results. The decline continued.

In 1998, the congregation tried a new way to address the issue. This predominantly Caucasian congregation of eight hundred members called a very distinguished African American minister, Alvin Jackson, from the eight-thousand-member Mississippi Boulevard Christian Church in Memphis, Tennessee, to be the minister. Jackson and the congregation's key leaders dreamed not of a Caucasian, Hispanic, or African American fellowship, but of a multicultural, multiracial, inclusive community of faith in the midst of the nation's capital.

Four months into the pastorate of the new senior minister, a strategic planning process was under way. The congregants were already catching on to a new way to think of their longstanding hospitality ministry: "A Church in the Heart of the City with a Heart for the City." Worship attendance was up by one half. Sunday visitors reflect the congregation's desire to be more representative of the rainbow of human differences. No racial or ethnic group seems to be the majority. The bulletin announced the upcoming potluck picnic for the gay/lesbian fellowship as well as the week's schedule for worship and study in Spanish. Only a handful of long-term members expressed their displeasure by leaving the faith community. A sense of joy and hopefulness fills the building on Sunday morning.

While far too early to declare victory, the signs are positive. The congregation's leaders have an exciting vision of where they want to be and what they want to do. They believe this to be a faithful response to God's leading. The congregation has direction and momentum.

Interpreting this vision with theological integrity will be the key to whether or not the congregation achieves it. In one sense, National City Christian Church attempts something radically new. If they succeed in becoming a multiracial, multicultural fellowship that harmoniously welcomes and celebrates diversity, the congregants will have, by God's grace, crossed over the rainbow. However, as Jackson explained, the congregants understand that the roots of this vision go deep into who they have always been. In one sense, they may seem to chart a new direction. In a different sense, however, they continue their ministry of hospitality in a direction consistent with their history. After all, Lyndon Johnson and James Garfield, key personalities in their story, believed in the oneness of the human community and advocated civil rights. The present vision continues that tradition. Even though not toward the same racial and cultural groups, they intend to target roughly the same socioeconomic constituency. Worship will become less formal and more participatory, but changes will be made within a traditional paradigm. The vision does not require National City to write a new story about itself. Instead, it is writing what it hopes will be several new, positive chapters to its old story.

A noted business leader could have been referring to Alvin Jackson and the pulpit committee of National City Christian Church when he said, "Leaders are painters of the vision and architects of the journey."

61

Renewing Congregations Have Leaders of Vision

In the book *The Color of Water*, James McBride tells of his mother pushing him toward the ministry. "You ever think about that?" she asked. "But you need foresight. And vision. You got vision?" McBride tells her he does not think he does. She responds emphatically. "Well, if you don't have it, don't waste God's time."[1]

Rachel McBride, James's mother, understands who and what it takes. As one noted business leader put it, "The leader's job is to create a vision."[2] Without an agreed-upon destination and a strategy to get there, the people experience church as little more than a series of unrelated study, worship, and outreaching activities strung together by pleasant conversations on quasi-religious topics. Random activity, even when well-intentioned, does little to affect the kingdom of God. Indeed, "where there is no vision, the people perish."[3]

In my study, I found that leadership not only needs to understand the congregation's story, but also must know how to connect that narrative self-understanding of present and past to a vision of where the congregation needs to head.

Effective leaders tend the vision, but they do not create it *ex nihilo*. They understand we worship the God who brings into being things far greater than we could ever imagine on our own. Consequently, responsible ministry can act on the assumption that God embeds in the congregation threads of what God envisions for the people. Rather than taking total responsibility for creating it, leadership teases the components of vision from the present congregation, with care to remember the congregation's distinctive story, then weaves them into a tapestry the congregation both believes is faithful to God and exciting to them. A meaningful next chapter in the congregation's story contains a vision of the possible.

The vision must be kept constantly before the people. Many ministers preach regularly on the congregation's vision statement. That keeps it fresh in the minds of the people. Frequently, the vision statement is displayed prominently in the fellowship hall, gathering area, sanctuary, or narthex. One church not only publishes "The Vision of This Church" on the front of the worship bulletin, but each new member is asked in the presence of the worshiping community to support the vision. "Will you introduce people to Jesus in positive ways? Will you become part of a Wesley Fellowship Group? Will you commit yourself to working to relieve suffering in this community and in the world?"

Vision Defined

Vision offers a dream of future possibility. While honoring the past and valuing the present, it brings focus to a realistic, credible, attractive destination at which the congregation can aim. Think of vision as a picture of a preferred future. The founding of America illustrates political vision casting at its best. The United States began in discontent. English rule, the colonists believed, could be improved. This sense of frustration eventually grew into a dream about what this country might be. That dream gave shape to ideas that ran deep in the American mythology. Our founders called for a nation where ordinary people had full opportunity to pursue more fulfilling lives. Eventually, a clear direction with well-defined values took shape. The American people rallied behind the hope and committed themselves to a strategy. Through trial, error, and struggle, this nation continues to move the possibility toward reality.

Renewing a congregation's ministry follows a similar process. It begins with the uneasy feeling that the people of God can do better. Too many congregations languish in the clutches of the status quo. Maintaining things the way they have always been may even constitute the only reason for being. Because the status quo offers no pull toward a meaningful goal, at best, apathy abounds. Unfortunately, pettiness often substitutes for the pursuit of purpose.[4]

Uneasiness about the present holds the potential for a new start. Leadership facilitates that process by probing: "What do we want our church to be like in the future?" "What does God call us to be and do?" "What gifts has God given this congregation that will permit us to be what God calls us to be?" Asking the right questions in the right way helps the congregation see the bridge between the present and the future.

The minister usually takes responsibility for encouragement and enthusiasm. Many tall-steeple ministers thoroughly understand the cheerleader dimension of their work. Some make the governing board meeting seem like a pep rally. By definition, leadership must be optimistic and passionate about the cause. After all, few fires start with wet matches.

As the vision takes shape, determination builds. Energy erodes malaise. Clarity about direction replaces vague disease. The emerging common vision begins to pull people out of the morass of bickering by challenging them to do more than work on their personal agendas. An enthusiastically accepted vision begins to renew spiritual health.

Offering a glimpse into an imagined tomorrow both

affects the present and jump-starts the future by energizing the skills, talents, and resources needed to move the present reality toward a future possibility. Henry Ford's vision of an affordable car and Steve Jobs's vision of a desktop personal computer attracted investment dollars and galvanized creative people who helped push and tug these visions toward reality.[5] Talented people in business, education, and government want to be in the midst of the action. Faith communities work the same way. Capable leaders, by painting the future as an improvement over the present, show God's people where to find the action in the church and what to do when they find it.

The congregation's dream must, of course, be faithful, credible, realistic, exhilarating, and inviting as well as connected to the community's sacred story. "To be the church we were in 1952" might attract a following, but can never be realistically convincing. We minister at the dawn of the twenty-first century. Therefore our plans for tomorrow must take into account the growing loss of confidence in reason, the sexual revolution of the past half century, the decline of the nuclear family, the end of Eurocentrism, the proliferation of diversity, and a host of other critical issues. God has provided us interesting times in which to live.

Planners must also remember that the congregational vision more resembles a watercolor than a snapshot. As the non-biblical proverb holds, "Give the divine a laugh. Tell God your plans." We cannot perfectly plan for the future because we cannot see it perfectly. We see only "in a mirror, dimly" (1 Cor. 13:12 NRSV). We catch glimpses, make assumptions, and take guesses as to what might be.

We do not, however, offer a watercolor vision without some hints of what the future holds. Richard Hamm, general minister and president of the Christian Church (Disciples of Christ), suggests that whatever else tomorrow might hold, we can be reasonably certain that healthy future congregations will demonstrate a passion for justice, model true caring community, and practice a deep Christian spirituality.[6] There is nothing new about the call for building local faith communities on the constructs of justice, community, and spirituality. Those criteria are the keys to mainline Protestant self-understanding.

We strain to hear a word from the Lord as to how to renew faith communities. We listen sensitively to God's people, set a tentative direction, keep the congregation reminded of the proposed destination, and shout encouragement—"Let's go! God calls us to a faithful future."

Whence Comes a Vision

I find Washington, D.C., to be an impressive city. It has beautifully planned parks, an intriguing street layout, and magnificent monuments. The city's sights overwhelm the average tourist, who asks, "How did the architects, planners, and artists think of all these different things? This land was once nothing more than a swamp of vacant lots, weeds, and woods."

The city began as the dream of visionaries. Each monument, museum, and building had its genesis in imagination. Not infrequently a concept was met with resistance, even ridicule. Effective dreamers valued and practiced persistence. They shared the vision until it resonated with others. They built support for the idea. They pushed legislation, raised funds, battled the opposition, broke ground, and they stayed with the dream until it became a reality.

A church, like a city, begins as a visionary's dream. The Country Club Christian Church in Kansas City worships in a magnificent Gothic building complete with American-styled grinning gargoyles. The founders were people of great vision. From the first day of his ministry, the organizing pastor expected the church to grow into one of the city's largest.[7] Early church board minutes report that the initial drawings were returned to the architect with instructions to make the sanctuary "ten feet wider and a little longer." They believed, "If we build it, God will bless us and they will come." A few years after completion, the sanctuary each Sunday morning was filled with people excited to be part of a dream becoming reality.

The recipe for vision includes one part foresight, one part insight, plenty of imagination, and a healthy dose of chutzpa. Combine these four ingredients with a sensitive awareness of the values, history, and culture of the congregation as well as ample knowledge of emerging ecclesiastical and social trends. Mix these in open minds while keeping hearts open to God's leading.

A vision differs from a pipe dream in that it builds on solid information and experience. The three-hundred-member congregation that built a thousand-seat sanctuary in the midst of an empty neighborhood knew the housing developer's bulldozers were scheduled to put in streets. The congregation's leaders had sufficient facts to convince a lending institution to fund their vision.

The Pastor as Resourcer of the Vision

Most of the leadership literature maintains that the one in charge of leading the institution takes responsibility for vision-building. A congregation's polity and history may expect and permit the minister this role. Roy Stauffer pastors the Lindenwood Christian Church in Memphis, Tennessee. In 1987, he preached a sermon envisioning the congregation's ministry for the next twenty-five years. The plan grew from his knowledge of the people, their values and history, as well as what he perceived as God's calling. The sermon found fertile ground in that faith community. A Long-range Planning Committee was appointed to guide the plan toward reality. The pastor kept the picture before the people. It became their action plan for mission and ministry.

Ten years later, Stauffer reported on the progress toward achieving the vision.[8] The congregation's ministry had expanded to include a day care center, pastoral counseling staff, after-school ministry for neighborhood children, plus a health and nutrition center. The congregation remodeled the building by modernizing offices, opening a memorial garden, and adding an art gallery and a visitors' center.

The pastor also kept the vision before the people by reminding them of goals yet to be accomplished before 2012, the end of the twenty-five-year plan. These included building a retirement center, a nursing home, and an endowment to sustain the ministry of the church. A reconstituted Long-range Planning Committee was assigned the task of moving these objectives toward reality.

Roy Stauffer illustrates the pastor as vision-caster. Frequently, circumstances or polity prevent the minister from assuming the role of visionary. On occasion, the minister lacks the foresight, creativity, organizational skills, or persistence to gather a vision. Fortunately, other methods exist. When the minister cannot do the job, find another way.

The Consultant as Facilitator of the Vision

Some congregations prefer outside leadership. This can be supplied by the denomination or middle judicatory, a well-trained pastor from a neighboring congregation, a professional church consultant, or the staff of a not-for-profit agency in the community that specializes in planning. Outside authorities offer advantages. To the pastor or congregation in short supply, the outsider can offer insight, intuition, and expertise. Some congregations give more authority to outsiders than to their own leadership. Outsiders also bring visioning experience. Outside consultation involves cost. Some tall steeples spend large sums of money on this. Smaller congregations, however, need not rule out this possibility. Fees need not be exorbitant.

On Occasion, Congregational Leadership Casts a Vision

Some congregations have enormously creative lay leadership. A task force of these people can sometimes successfully pull a vision together. They need resources,[9] guidance, and a heavy dose of the Holy Spirit, but it can be done. Rod Wilmoth at Minneapolis's Hennepin Avenue United Methodist Church reports that their lay leadership pulled much of the vision together before he was appointed senior minister. On his arrival and with his final input, the plan was completed.

Rarely, however, does a vision emerge this way. Vision tends to take root in dissatisfaction. Long-range Planning Committees usually consist of people pleased with the present operation. Worldly-wise clergy understand the risk in calling attention to discontent with the way things are. By their nature, people who cast effective visions long to make the future better, not to defend the present. When either contented people or those fearful of risk take charge of planning, future projections usually seek a replication of the present. Because the next chapter of the congregation's story must, by definition, differ from the last, be careful in trying to make visioning an ordinary committee process.

69

Try Putting a Group in Charge of Disrupting Present Thinking

Doing so may make it possible for a committee of members to glimpse a vision that differs from the present. Consider the congregation that admitted to a great love for the status quo. The same pictures always hung on the same walls, in the same places. One young mother pointed out that the newsletter announcing her baby's birth was worded identically to her birth announcement twenty-seven years previously. The congregation saw little necessity for change. Per capita stewardship declined, but the congregation managed to keep expenses within its income. Attendance had been dropping for a decade, but so slowly that few people took notice. The average age of congregants nudged into the low sixties, but a few young adults joined every year. Attempts to change anything met strong, even angry, resistance. "If it's not broken, don't fix it."

The minister and a visionary lay leader stumbled on an idea that broke open existing ways of thinking and doing to make room for renewal to take place. They appointed a Future Focus Committee to function as the congregation's "think tank." This group was assigned to read cutting-edge literature on the post-establishment church in a postmodern world and report the findings to the church board.

Initially, neither the congregation nor the Future Focus Committee understood the purpose. Committees normally have more agenda than time to think, read, and deliberate. The first year, the Future Focus Committee reviewed and discussed twenty-five books on change in mainline Protestantism. In time, a pattern emerged. They selected a topic, for example, "How to Reach the Younger Generation" or "Better Ways to Govern the Local Congregation." After thorough research and discussion, the committee wrote a five- to ten-page position paper and distributed it to congregational leadership. The committee members began to call themselves "The Tree Toppers." The name came from their responsibility to watch the horizons of change and tell those slogging through the swamp of the present what they saw coming. The Future Focus chairperson became a regular on the agenda of the church board. Some of the more controversial reports were circulated through the entire congregation.

As the congregation moved to develop and adopt a vision, the Future Focus Committee made valuable contributions to the discussion. They knew what the "experts" were saying. Their reports already had the congregation thinking about issues the planning process surfaced. The Future Focus Committee opened the congregation to new ways of thinking by challenging old ways of doing.

Whatever It Takes, Do It

Vision comes from God. It can be midwifed by an individual, a consultant, lay leaders, the minister, a Future Focus Committee, a long-range planning process, or any combination of the above. The visioning process may be systematic, or it may prove messy. Congregations differ. Leaders respond to their unique setting by doing whatever it takes to get the job done.

The pastor assumes responsibility for tending the vision. The task never concludes. Present ministry requires constant evaluation in light of changing circumstances. The leader continually scans the horizon for new developments and formulates tentative plans for responding when and if they become realities. Because organizations tend to forget, the minister keeps the people reminded about where they are headed. Vision casting, quite simply, has the permanency of writing the evening news in a snowbank during a blizzard. It must be redone continually lest it be lost from sight. It must also be revised continually lest it be rendered irrelevant.

A conference held some years ago at Cambridge University sought to answer the question "What causes certain people to become visionaries?" They discovered that these people live as though they see another world. Even while in this world, their actions are governed by the other world.[10] Another writer suggests, these people live under the influence of what they envision. They shatter the reality of their own time by operating in the present as though the future has come.[11]

Unfortunately, not all visions mobilize for good. Like Moses and Jesus, Joseph Stalin and Adolph Hitler imagined what they considered a better future, gathered people around the vision, and worked to make it happen. The minister must always be concerned to ask, "Is this what God calls us to do?" As John Killinger reminds us, visionaries "should learn to see the world of God's envisioning a world of happiness, justice, peace, and sharing, a world where the lion and the lamb can lie side by side in perfect harmony of spirit."[12]

THE IMPORTANCE OF PLANNING AND IMPLEMENTING

Saint Lucas United Church of Christ

Saint Louis, Missouri

Saint Lucas United Church of Christ sits on the edge of Saint Louis, Missouri. Within a mile or two, an exclusive private school nestles behind a long stone fence. Abutting the church's property are $300,000 to $400,000 homes.

The facility, like the spelling of the name, reflects its origin as a faith community for people of German descent. The frequently expanded stone building suggests sturdiness rather than ostentation. Everything, including the large parish cemetery on the property, is immaculate, maintained, trimmed, and substantial.

Gary Clark, senior minister since 1995, was ordained a United Methodist minister and transferred his ordination into the United Church of Christ. Even though he did not grow up with the Evangelical and Reformed traditions of Saint Lucas, he shares the penchant for Teutonic scrupulosity and extends it to pastoral ministry. He could put a sign on his desk claiming, "I project. I plan. I implement." As a testimony to the systematic application of caring skills, on his office wall hangs a bulletin board listing the names of eighty elderly members and how often the staff has visited them in the past year.

Clark began our conversation by telling the congregation's story: "Let's back up and take in some history. The congregation was founded in 1880. Vegetable farming dominated the area until sixty years ago. Then the city of Saint Louis began to grow this way, and we grew with it."

Clark traced the congregation's ups and downs through the last half century. He told of a predecessor who "walked the alleys, trailer parks, and suburban streets knocking on doors, introducing himself and inviting people to Saint Lucas Church."

The narration meandered into a reference about personnel difficulties in the past decade. Fortunately, the congregation's able matriarchs and patriarchs stepped forward to hold things together. Although the long-term members were not in official places of leadership, as the minister explained, the congregation trusted and relied on them.

Following an effective interim ministry, the people willingly handed over the mantle of leadership to Clark. The lay leaders said, "Dr. Clark, you just tell us what we need to do." He accounted for the ease with which the people extended him their trust. "The congregation had one hundred eighteen years of history. One hundred six of those years have been very good."

Clark began his ministry by making a careful assessment of the circumstances. Although the membership appeared as a marching band scrambling to change formations, three critical issues were identified. Clark developed a strategy to address each.

First, the congregation had a poor self-image. Clark reported, "People actually asked me if I thought the church could survive. I told them that we have more than a hundred years of great mission history. We have a large number of members (eighteen hundred at the time). We will not only survive, we will thrive."

He went on to describe the strategy. "I decided we

74

should address feelings of low self-esteem by celebrating every positive thing that happened. Today, we incorporate celebration into all we do. A group of older members were so discouraged by declining numbers that they decided to disband and give their treasury to the church. I attended one of their meetings and asked them to remember all the positive contributions they had made to the church. They recounted so many wonderful experiences together that they decided to reorganize and head in a new direction. Now they have a new mission and a renewed energy. At Saint Lucas, we celebrate every good thing!"

Second, the congregation had a recent history of using the endowment funds to pay general expenses. "I responded with a strong stewardship emphasis," Clark reported. "I preach about it and teach about it. We do effective stewardship campaigns. We rewrote the endowment policy to keep ourselves from spending those funds on regular expenses. We have also adopted a 'full disclosure' policy on finances. In three years we went from red ink to $100,000 in a reserve fund. Remarkable results, I'd say."

Third, "We needed to build program. I addressed that by making changes in staff assignments. We also conducted a retreat for lay leaders at which increased-program need was discussed. Since then, the congregation's program life has been significantly enriched."

The new minister's intentional planning and implementing had significant results. Saint Lucas United Church of Christ currently enjoys the highest annual giving and average worship attendance in its one-hundred-twenty-year history.

Make It Happen: Translate Vision into Reality

Vision requires a strategy for translating the idea into reality. As *Fortune Magazine*'s Tom Stewart puts it, "Don't just preach the vision, manage it." Consequently, there must be "a plan." All vital tall-steeple churches have a blueprint for accomplishing what they set out to do. Sometimes a formal planning process produces a notebook for distribution. At other times, an informal process produces a report written only in the minds and hearts of the people. Sometimes the senior minister develops the plan. Sometimes the lay leadership does. At Hennepin Avenue United Methodist in Minneapolis, the plan was developed by both. The lay leadership completed much of a strategic plan process before the new senior minister arrived. He had the responsibility to confirm the direction, complete the details, and put the plan into action. At First United Methodist in Peoria, Illinois, the senior minister unpacked his vision, and a plan grew up around it during a full first year of preaching and teaching. It took another four years for the congregation to integrate the plan fully into their ways of thinking and doing. At Bay Presbyterian Church, Bay Village, Ohio, it took ten years to develop formal vision and mission statements and a long-range plan. The minister devoted most of the first decade of his tenure to resolving staff issues and building spiritual momentum. At Saint Lucas United Church of Christ, Gary Clark took responsibility for developing the initial strategy in response to the circumstances he found. Only after restoring the congregation's self-confidence has he started to engage the faith community in the formal process of developing a comprehensive plan. Every congregation does things differently. However, all have some sort of strategy that guides them.

Every tall-steeple leader establishes vision and implements the plan differently. Some are very analytical and intentional. They articulate precisely what they do and why they do it. They quote literature on change management and conflict resolution. They read Peter Drucker as well as the apostle Paul. Consequently, they can cite chapter and verse for a theologically integrated explanation of their leadership process.

On the other hand, some very capable leaders seem to have few analytical skills and no particular insight into church management. The reason for their congregation's vibrancy may even puzzle them. They rely on intuition rather than analysis. Still other clergy combine intuition and analytical skills with an intentional planning process. Without exception, however, vital tall steeples' leaders have some method for making it happen. They translate vision into reality.

Some Leaders Develop a Strategic Plan

Strategic planning appeals to some congregations. Their ministers appreciate how this extensive and complex planning process requires significant input from many church members. Consequently, when finished, it has wide acceptance. The congregation does not need to be sold on the plan. The people already believe it is theirs. Lay leaders frequently advocate for strategic planning because it has a positive track record in the business community.

Strategic planning begins by identifying needs, trends, expectations, and resources. It proceeds to develop tactics for moving the vision from possibility to reality, assigns responsibility, evaluates effectiveness, and then begins the process all over again. Strategic planning can be done in different ways. Each variant, however, depends on asking, answering, and following up on certain basic questions. All of these questions help clarify a congregation's distinctive story, link that story to the vision, and then build a strategy for moving into the future.

- *The Profile Questions:* Where are we now? How did we get here? What is our history? What do we believe? What basic, core values represent our church?
- *The Missional Questions:* What do we do? What purpose do we serve? What mission does our church have?
- *The External Evaluation Questions:* What outside the church affects us? How does the community affect our mission and ministry? What do people expect of us? What strengths and weaknesses do other churches in the community have? What religious needs does our community not presently meet? What do other people in the community think of us?
- *The Internal Evaluation Questions:* What inside our congregation affects how and what we plan? How well do we presently fulfill our mission? What strengths and weaknesses does our congregation have? Are clergy, staff, laity, and membership open to new ideas and ways of doing?
- *The Vision Questions:* Where do we want to be? Given this assessment of who we are and where we have been, for what future do we plan?
- *The Strategic Plan Questions:* How do we get there? In this analysis of who we are, what we do, and what affects us, what critical issues have surfaced that must be addressed? What objectives, goals, and strategies, if

78

enacted, will take us where we want to go? How do we calendar strategy and assign responsibility?

- *The Evaluative Questions:* How did we do? Did we accomplish what we set out to do? How do we celebrate our accomplishments? How do we correct for our failings?

Unfortunately, It Is Not That Simple

Many, if not most, approaches to strategic planning present the process as a cookbook recipe to be followed closely.

Take two parts of congregational survey on present needs and attitudes. Mix with one part community resource assessment. Stir in the agreed-upon list of core values. Strain through the minds of a committee assigned to write the mission statement. Marinate in focus group discussions on critical issues facing the community and congregation. Let simmer in the imagination of the most creative leaders until an unmistakable vision floats to the surface. Season to local tastes. Bake until a strategy becomes self-evident. When sufficiently cooked, tasks divide naturally into objectives and underlying goals. Slice into bite-sized action plans. Serve until every responsibility has been assumed. Rejoice when achieving the vision. Make necessary corrections for weaknesses. When finished, start the process all over again.

Would that it be so simple. Strategic planning by recipe assumes organizations behave rationally and predictably.[1] Unfortunately, "predictable" and "intelligent" seldom describe day-to-day life in any organization. Consequently, in recent years, the business community's confidence in the recipe approach to planning has declined so drastically that one of the significant management books of the 1990s was *The Rise and Fall of Strategic Planning.*[2]

Congregations encounter the same problem with recipe planning. Hidden, historical, subjective, multifarious factors embedded in church life stymie attempts at straightforward cause-effect planning. Leonard Sweet catches the essence of the problem: "The notion that leaders can plot strategies that will guide their institutions safely into the future is as stupid as the five bridesmaids' belief that they could predict when the bridegroom will arrive."[3] How simple the work of ministry would be if we did not have to account for people and their personal as well as collective faith journeys.

Think of strategic planning as a tool, not a magic pill. Do not expect spiritual renewal to spring naturally from a well-executed strategic planning process. This does not mean, however, that the church should not plan. Our Lord rightly admonished those who try to build a tower without a plan for finishing it (Luke 14:28-30).

In my study, I found vital congregations that engaged in strategic planning. Some hired outside consultants. Others used trained members of their congregations. When their plans were complete, some adhered very closely to them. Others found the process more valuable than the actual plan.

Most Congregations Plan Less Formally

The senior minister and church governing board frequently invent a planning process that works for their congregation. At Saint Lucas in Saint Louis, the new minister did not wait for a congregation process. He simply designed the first run at a plan. In the fourth year of his ministry, he began to involve lay leadership in the development of a long-range plan. This pattern is more typical than developing a strategic plan. At times it works as well as strategic planning. On other occasions, it is not nearly as effective. Regardless, it is a plan.

A Plan Where There Seems to Be None

Some ministers have little understanding of plans, strategies, or analyses and still pastor vital congregations. A publication on growing churches featured the mission and ministry of a particularly effective congregation. The long-term senior minister was very honest. "When you read that history, you get the feeling that we had a plan for what we did. You might even assume I knew what I was doing. There was no formal plan. We have been very blessed, but it isn't because I understood what we needed to do."

Another minister led his congregation through difficulty after difficulty into a time of profound effectiveness without any evidence of having any technical understanding of conflict resolution, visioning, or planning. He has difficulty explaining or even admitting to his effectiveness.

Similiar accounts abound. Vital congregations can develop with leaders who do not articulate reasonable explanations for what they do or how they do it. When asked for an explanation, they often shrug and offer a theological response: "It has been by God's grace." Others report using personal spiritual retreats to discern God's leading. Still others offer a psychological explanation for how they do what they do: "I just knew in my bones what would work, and I set about to do it. I am a highly intuitive person." Obviously, a loving God operates through intuition as well as the science of management.

Take note, however, that even though highly intuitive ministers do not have a formal, written plan, they have a process by which to translate vision into reality. It may be "I just have a feeling about what to do," but they keep the congregation moving.

Governance: The Machinery by Which the Church Operates

Tall-steeple church governments can be enormous. One congregation spends several hundred dollars each year just to research and publish an "Organizational Flow Chart." More than three hundred people serve on the church's governing board, twenty-three standing committees, and more than a dozen task forces. In that church, just keeping the ecclesiastical machinery greased approaches a full-time job.

Every congregation has some sort of governance system to involve the people of the faith community in developing and implementing the plan. Although governance differs in nomenclature and methodology, most require large numbers of laity to serve on an array of committees, councils, and boards.

Many, if not most, of the congregations I visited find the traditional methods of ordering their life inadequate. They complain that too many meetings and terms of service that are too long have shallowed the pool of willing volunteers. Local church government, like Washington bureaucracy, has become too big and too cumbersome. Consequently, many vital tall steeples seek to simplify their governance systems. Often this means reducing the size and meeting frequency of governing bodies.

Church governance is undergoing fundamental change. In the last generation, when most governing systems were designed, committees, boards, and councils functioned to assimilate new members and keep long-term ones active. "We used to say," one minister told me, "put him on the board. It will get him involved." Most people experienced church governance as pleasant discussions where an occasional vote was taken. The church meeting was considered ministry in and of itself. With that understanding, lay leadership seldom objected to a three-hour meeting where the most important agenda item established a date for the next meeting.

That has changed. Governance now seeks to get people involved in ministry, not to be their ministry. Therefore people expect church government to set policy, establish ministry programs, and make wise decisions as quickly as possible. This seldom requires a monthly meeting of a two-hundred-member church board micromanaging daily activities.

Although often restricted by denominational polity, vital tall steeples struggle to streamline their governance structure to make it more responsive. Translating a vision into reality demands effective governance.

Good Planning Builds Support
Every Step of the Way

"Why doesn't that house look as nice as the others in the neighborhood?" a child asked her father. "The garage door has a broken window. The paint is chipping. The roof has a loose shingle. Why don't the people who live there keep it up?"

Mustering all his fatherly wisdom, he tried to explain. "The people who own the house don't live there. They live in another state. The people who live there only rent the house. They don't feel that it belongs to them. If those who owned it lived there, or if those who lived there owned it, I think the house would get better treatment."

The generalization about rental property applies to

church life. The less ownership people feel, the less likely they are to give wholehearted support. Certainly, they will not be as enthusiastic as they will if they think it belongs to them. The most effective leaders of tall-steeple churches apply this principle. They do not dictate the vision or the plan. They build support every step of the way. They preach and teach and encourage and explain constantly.

The vision may come from God. The plan may be the most creative ever written. However, if the people do not own it, not much happens.

A PLACE THAT SETS HIGH EXPECTATIONS

Peachtree Presbyterian Church

Atlanta, Georgia

In the depth of the Great Depression the property of Atlanta's Peachtree Presbyterian Church was sold on the courthouse steps. The financially strapped congregation failed to meet the interest obligation on a $40,000 loan. Since that inauspicious moment in 1936, Peachtree has grown to become the largest local faith community of the Presbyterian Church (USA). The financial wolf no longer howls outside the door. In the past twenty-five years, the congregation has given over $100 million for mission, ministry, and capital, with over 50 percent of non-designated giving going "to others."[1]

The church is located on the edge of one of Atlanta's residential areas, not far from a complex of high-rise office buildings and finer shopping centers. As might be anticipated, this congregation does everything in a big way. Many clergy dream of serving in a city with as many residents as Peachtree Presbyterian has members. The church's 1996 income exceeded $13 million. The church spent $600,000 for a television ministry. (Some claim that at almost any time of the day or night a Peachtree Presbyterian worship service will be on at least one cable station.) Due to extremely limited on-site parking, the church spends $169,000 annually for charter buses to bring worshipers from commercial parking lots. The winter/spring activities catalog runs to eighty pages and describes several hundred opportunities for service and study.

Peachtree Presbyterian attracts sufficient young adults that the congregation's median age hovers around the national average. The church's large number of younger visitors promises an even lower average age in the future. To accommodate its continuing growth, the congregation added another 110,000 square feet, at a cost of $16 million, to an already large facility. Not only does this congregation make a strong witness in the present, it is poised for a significant future.

Each week more than five thousand people attend one of the three, nearly identical, very traditional Sunday morning worship services. These services feature a pipe organ, robed choirs, and a Presbyterian liturgy done "decently and in good order." An attempt was made at a more contemporary worship celebration, but attracted only a small following. "Boomer" and "GenX" clergy on staff continue to call for an alternative service, but a convincing case has yet to be made.

When I asked Steve Bacon, minister for administration and stewardship, the secret of this congregation's vitality, he responded instantly: "The church has flourished because Frank Harrington has been the senior minister for nearly three decades." Bacon, an associate minister, explained that Harrington, the senior minister, excels as both preacher and leader. His sermons for daily living pack the pews weekly. He offers the visionary leadership needed to build a large, healthy institution. Bacon explained further by saying that Harrington's deep commitment to congregational growth manifests itself through intentional planning. People, as Bacon reminded me, must plan their work and work their plan. Rather than micromanaging, Bacon believes Harrington's leadership style expects accountability to the vision, is offered with pastoral compassion, and demands the best everyone has to offer.[2]

Renewal Demands Excellence

Noted theologian John Cobb believes the decline of the mainline churches can be traced to the spiritual sickness of lukewarmness.[3] Institutions flourish, he notes, when their constituency commits passionately to their beliefs and values. The church expands only when Christian people organize their lives around the supreme importance of their faith. Unfortunately, mainline Protestants languish in a era when faith seldom breaks the Top Five list of priorities. As Dr. Cobb argues, we have become like the church in Laodicea, neither hot nor cold. Even when we share convictions, we express little excitement about them. As American slang states it, when it comes to matters of the mainline church, "Whatever."

Vital tall steeples counter this lukewarmness trend. They demonstrate fervor for the faith. Curiously, their passion has a distinctive mainline twist. They manifest it by setting high standards for ecclesiastical operations. The demand for excellence in program and facilities as well as mission and ministry characterizes the vital tall steeples.

One highly effective pastor offered insight into why the emphasis is placed on organizational and institutional excellence: "I know the Bible teaches that we are saved by grace through faith. My experience, however, is that this grace comes through the church of Jesus Christ. It may be heresy, but I believe I was saved by the church. For this reason, I love the church. I would give my life to the church. I will always give the church the very best I have to offer."

Few, I suspect, want to wade into that theological morass. However, the leaders of vital tall steeples, both laity and clergy, approach being compulsive about the quality of everything done by the local church. They believe that any shoddy presentation demeans the church of Jesus Christ. This striving for excellence can be seen in everything from cared-for buildings with manicured lawns and immaculately polished linoleum hallways to well-written brochures announcing forthcoming events to work standards ministers set for themselves to the accountability they demand from others. In everything, these congregations believe the proclamation of the gospel demands excellence. James Moore, Saint Luke's United Methodist in Houston, said, "I tell our people, 'There must be some church in the world where they do everything right.' Then I encourage them to believe we can be that church."

Neatness May Not Be Everything, But It Counts

In spite of a midtown, urban core location on Main Street, First Presbyterian Church, Houston, Texas, has the environmental "feel" of a neighborhood church. Its large facility invites rather than overwhelms. Towering oak trees partially conceal the enormity of the building. The precision-trimmed, manicured lawn interfaces clean-swept sidewalks. Church flower beds are maintained as meticulously as those in the nearby museum district. The grounds of First Presbyterian look like an English garden. They send a clear message: "This place is loved. The people who attend here will love you as well. Please join us."

Many church buildings send a different message. A slovenly appearance says, "We do not care much about this place. We may not even care much about you." Congregations do not intend that message. It comes from an ecclesiastical edifice malady known as "Junked Up Syndrome." Congregants too often let the building's outside deteriorate. On the inside, outdated Sunday school materials collect on tables. Old pianos accumulate in the storeroom. Hallways show the wear of decades without fresh paint. The wax builds at the edge of the floors. The people may love the church and one another. However, they permit their facility to become "visitor repelling." The frequent users do not even notice the clutter. The lack of cleanliness drifts beyond their awareness. Since the regular membership needs no directing, it does not notice the lack of signs. Visitors must explore in order to find the sanctuary, the parking lot, or the church office. The members and their leaders seldom ask what message their building sends.

At Houston's First Presbyterian, the care given the outside extends to the interior. Hallways shine like mirrors. Walls show no scuff marks. Display tables are organized. Even in the midst of a $15 million renovation, the building is used to the maximum. On the Tuesday afternoon I visited, the place was a beehive of activity. Children's laughter could be heard in the halls. Parents lined the driveway dropping off and picking up their little ones. Classrooms buzzed with adults learning and fellowshipping. In spite of the crowds and the construction, everything in and out of the building remains beautifully kept. This congregation believes the facility sends a message about the importance of the faith as well as the institution.

Eric Hoffer, the populist longshoreman philosopher whose fifteen minutes of fame came more than thirty years ago, believed a positive correlation exists between societal health and building maintenance. He contended that vital institutions can be identified by well-swept floors and a nail on which to hang the broom. While clean floors do not create institutional health, he insisted, they do indicate its presence.

When Hoffer made that comment on a television talk show in 1969, I thought it was silly. Now I wonder if he might have been onto something. Certainly, it fits with the practices of vital tall steeples. They believe neatness counts for something. They do it. Their buildings are immaculate and their lawns well-groomed. Their visitors' information tables are well-stocked and neat. The bulletin boards are up-to-date.

Large congregations have no natural immunity to "Junked Up Syndrome." Like small- and medium-sized congregations, they can let their buildings slide into environmental neglect. Several leaders related how they continually preach, "If it's cluttered, straighten it up. If it's dirty, clean it. If it's broken, fix it. And whatever you do, don't step over a discarded cola can on the sidewalk. Pick it up and throw it in the trash can."

The Neatness Rule Has Exceptions

Park Avenue United Methodist Church, Minneapolis, was established in the 1920s in a neighborhood of elegant three-story homes. In the 1960s the surrounding area began a racial transition. Today the neighborhood is about one-third European American, one-half African American, with several other groups making up the final sixth.

The congregation found ways to embrace the change. Twenty-five years ago, Park Avenue Church sponsored a summer "Soul Liberation Festival" on the church's parking lot. Open-air gospel music and preaching bounced off the houses and echoed down the streets. The invited neighbors responded. A grand time was had by all. A tradition was born. Today, the congregation sponsors the Park Avenue Urban Summer Ministry, which draws hundreds of children and adults into an incredibly diverse offering of study and recreational activities. In addition, Cornerstone Ministries, the church's ministry extension into the neighborhood, offers a free medical clinic, free legal help, and a food bank.

The congregation reflects the racial makeup of the neighborhood. Worship service music mixes traditional and classical with contemporary praise music, gospel, and even an occasional rap. In the service I attended, the choir, itself a rainbow of colors, followed an African American spiritual with a selection from Handel's *Messiah*. Park Avenue United Methodist offers a positive model of mission and ministry for racial reconciliation.

One cannot, however, say that this congregation gets overly concerned about its building's appearance. Cream-colored paint curls off the ceilings. The leaking roof has been repaired, but the resultant crumbling plaster has not been replaced. Every wall, window, floor, and door shows wear and tear. The building is clean, but not well-maintained. Rather than neglect or a simple lack of funding, maintenance slide seems to be intentional. The building's appearance sends a clear message to the congregation's constituency: "Bringing people of different backgrounds together is more important to us than painted walls."

Neatness neglect does not, however, indicate disinterest in excellence. Park Avenue United Methodist maintains very high standards. Well-prepared ministers and choirs lead a well-planned worship service. The summer ministry catalog was expensively printed. The program and class offerings reflect the congregation's pursuit of excellence. They set very high standards in everything except building maintenance.

Do Nothing Haphazardly

A conversation with Vic Pentz, the senior minister at Houston's First Presbyterian Church, demonstrated how vital churches push the expectation for excellence beyond clean hallways and weedless flower beds. "We must set high standards for the Lord's work. This is one of my obsessions." He went on to explain that while studying in Israel he saw an intensity of religious commitment that put to shame the secularized Christianity of this country. "When I had my fiftieth birthday, I recommitted myself to maintaining the highest standards. There is nothing more important than the work of the church. We cannot settle for less than the best." Another minister said, "A mistake in the Sunday worship bulletin will, of course, be forgiven. I will never accept, however, the attitude that those mistakes are unimportant. God never asks for more than our best. We should never be comfortable offering less."

The Basilica of Saint Mary, a Roman Catholic congregation in downtown Minneapolis, demonstrates that mainline Protestants have no corner on setting high standards. Built in the 1920s, the Basilica fell on hard times as its members moved out of the inner city. During this time of decline, the magnificent facility fell into such disrepair that plaster falling from the ceiling endangered liturgist and worshiper alike.

The parish is now undergoing a spectacular revival. In the past decade, the church has spent $9 million renovating the building. The membership has grown from nine hundred to forty-five hundred families! It used to be a congregation of the elderly. Now 70 percent of the membership is between twenty and forty. "A Traditional Church with a Modern Message" has become the motto.

Spokespersons for the Basilica attribute this renaissance to their efforts to live out a mission statement that emerged from a planning conference in the late 1980s: "The Basilica of Saint Mary has a four-fold mission: to provide *quality* [emphasis mine] liturgy, religious education, pastoral care, and hospitality; to preach justice and provide emergency relief to the poor; to pursue interfaith relationships; and to contribute to the cultural quality of this community. The

93

parish is marked by hospitality and a rich diversity of age, ethnic, racial, social, and economic backgrounds."

They take their pursuit of quality worship so seriously that "if a priest doesn't say the Mass well or doesn't read Scripture effectively, he is assigned to the least attended services. Sunday morning is reserved for those who do the job well."

This expectation for excellence permeates other ministries. A priest told of a young adult who told him, "I came to see the building and decided to stay for the liturgy. I continued to return because of the outreach this church has to the city and the opportunities offered for volunteering in ministry."

At Houston's Saint Luke's United Methodist Church, Jim Moore says, "We want to be able to tell every visitor about every program, 'It's just great.' If they ask, 'How's your music?' we need to say, 'Just great!' If they continue, 'What about Saint Luke's youth program?' we want to honestly reply, 'That too is just great.' As the senior minister, my job is to be constantly searching, planning, and pushing to make sure the gaps are filled and that we can say to every inquiry, 'That is just great.' "

Still another minister said, "I keep this message before the staff and the lay leadership: 'We are not activity directors in a resort community trailer park. We are trying to connect people to God's love in Jesus Christ. That requires the best we have.' "

The Best Over Time

Almost without exception, vital tall-steeple churches demonstrate an established pattern of long-tenured senior ministers. Frequently, the lead pastor of twenty years will have followed a twenty-year pastorate that followed a twenty-five-year ministry. This confirms common sense. Without stability in leadership, instability ensues. Few things, after all, can be accomplished quickly. As Calvin Coolidge put it, perhaps with more hyperbole than one might expect, "Nothing in the world can take the place of persistence. Persistence and determination alone are omnipotent. The slogan 'Press On' has solved and will always solve the problems of the human race."

Actually, ecclesiastical viability requires more than having a minister stay. Some congregations decline significantly during a long-term ministry. Leadership, particularly in the office of the senior minister, must offer the excellence that comes with being visionary, competent, *and* long-tenured.

A Price to Be Paid

The senior ministers of vital tall steeples tend to be competent, long-term leaders who set high standards, have vision, and understand how to translate that vision into reality. They also pay a price for the job they do. These positions are demanding. Most people enter ministry because they like to be liked and hate to be hated. Because we love people and appreciate their approval, we usually have a "thin skin." Consequently, we do not take unsolicited negative criticism well. Unfortunately, we all get it. The mantle of leadership comes with a target painted on the back. Stones come flying from the sidelines with regularity.

Senior ministers of the large congregations I surveyed report having to deal with far more negatives than they ever had in smaller congregations. The large-membership church may simply have a larger pool of complainants. The more visible CEO role of the lead pastor may invite critics. It may simply be that people feel as unrestrained in complaining about the "public pulpit preacher" as they do any other public person.

For whatever the reason, the senior ministers of large congregations must come to terms with this negative dimension of ministry. As one minister commented, "I used to maintain a file on anonymous letters. In this job, I need a filing cabinet. In previous pastorates I could please all of the people some of the time. Not true here. No matter what I do here, I am criticized. If I ever come close to pleasing everyone, someone will be angry because I did! Those things still hurt. However, accepting their inevitability set me free. I no longer worry about trying to please everyone. Instead, I strive to do what I believe is in the long-term best interest of this congregation. Instead of asking, 'What will help me avoid criticism?' I ask, 'What is God calling me to do?' "

The expectation for excellence extracts a price.

"MISSION IS WHY WE ARE HERE"[1]

Fourth Presbyterian Church

Chicago, Illinois

Chicago's Magnificent Mile on North Michigan Avenue sends a clear message of affluence and privilege. The John Hancock Center, the nation's fifth tallest building, looks down on department stores and boutiques where a man's necktie can be purchased for $100, and a woman's dress can cost as much as a good used car. Luxury condominiums occupy the top floors of high-rise buildings. The city's most elegant hotels charge visitors the equivalent of a monthly car payment for a night's lodging.

The gray limestone and magnificent Gothic architecture of Fourth Presbyterian Church fit into this neighborhood. Everything about the church confirms this was built as a religious community for the Windy City's movers and shakers. The pastor describes the congregation as "the people who aren't supposed to be there—busy, secular, goal-oriented, hardworking, mostly young city people."[2]

A few years ago, I attended worship at Fourth Presbyterian on a bitter cold January Sunday. The sanctuary filled from front to back with both ordinary Chicagoans and those the newspaper society editor calls "the city's beautiful people." This church fits on Chicago's North Michigan Avenue.

What a mistake, however, to conclude that either the church or the neighborhood stays isolated from the city's not-so-blessed. The homeless regularly check the trash cans near the church. Cabrini-Green lies one mile west of North Michigan Avenue. Thirteen thousand people struggle to survive in that public housing project that symbolizes everything gone wrong in America's urban policy.

Emil Brunner once observed, "The church exists by mission as fire exists by burning." Members of Fourth Presbyterian Church strive to live out their faith accordingly. As their pastor, John Buchanan, asserts, the congregation shapes its ministry with the understanding that mainline churches have an obligation to be in the world.

The congregants make mission a priority. Their partnership with Cabrini-Green takes church people into the project and brings project people into the church. They feed hungry people and tutor struggling children. The congregation also operates a community counseling program and a senior citizen center. The descriptions of Fourth Presbyterian's outreaching ministries run to a small book.

This congregation does not, however, simply "talk the talk," but "walks the walk." In the past few years, I have had opportunities to be in the building on a number of occasions weekdays. The hallways and classrooms of the church bustle with ministry being done with multitudes of Chicago's less fortunate. The church's size, location, and history make Fourth Presbyterian a model for reaching out to others. It is not alone. Most of the vital tall steeples I surveyed make mission a priority. Serving others is critical to mainline renewal.

Outreach Takes Priority in Renewing Mainlines

To be considered vital, a mainline faith community must offer more than great music, good feelings, and strong coffee. It takes more to renew a church than reversing membership decline, expanding fellowship opportunities, resolving all internal conflicts, and increasing worship attendance. To be healthy, a congregation must move people toward a passionate, mature faith.

While not a simple task to agree on what defines spiritual maturity, the Search Institute determined that a fully developed faith clusters around several dimensions.[3] The researchers reviewed the literature, consulted with scholars, and surveyed a broad spectrum of adults. Then they concluded that mature Christians are concerned about evangelism and social justice, pray regularly as well as advocate justice, consider biblical study and theological reflection lifelong processes, utilize the core teachings of their faith to shape daily decisions, and participate in a faith community through regular worship and fellowship.

The mainline congregations that continue to renew over long periods of time take seriously this richly textured understanding of spiritual maturity. They organize their community life around providing diverse opportunities for people to develop their faith. Healthy churches do not ask people to choose between evangelism and discipleship or between offering a prayer and working for social justice. They understand these simply as different moments in faith development and practice. Vital churches do Bible study, but also stress the application of biblical principles to life. They strive to teach people to think theologically, but also encourage them to act as though they think theologically. Vital churches never neglect greasing the wheels of congregational life. They do not, however, expend all their energy on the machinery of governance, facility upkeep, and encouraging new people to join. They "take care of the church," but they also set people free to get involved in mission beyond institutional maintenance.

The tall steeples I studied put particular emphasis on reaching out to others. They move ministry beyond the confines of Sunday morning worship. They discourage the notion that Christianity exists only as a state of heart or mind. These congregations lead people to put their faith in action.

Key to Developing Mission Program: Find a Need and Fill It

This dictum can be understood as the mantra for "consumer-driven megachurch management." If anyone asks for anything—casual worship, Saturday services, coffee breaks during the sermon, classes on astrological signs— give it to them. When that is taken to extremes, those with the least knowledge of the faith and least commitment to the church become determiners of ecclesiastical polity, procedure, and theology.

Vital mainline tall steeples respond to need, but resist succumbing to the worst aspects of the consumer-driven mentality. As one minister put it, "We find that when a church is designed to relate to people's needs, people respond. 'Find a need and fill it' is Robert Schuller's famous dictum, and we follow it with a passion . . . [but we also understand] . . . one of their needs is the need to serve others."[4]

100

The congregations I surveyed offer a multitude of avenues by which people serve others.

Mission by Checkbook Still Alive and Well

In the American culture, money carries enormous significance. Consequently, leading congregations value financing the church's mission. According to Herb Miller, effective large congregations put a "strong emphasis on world missions, benevolence, and community outreach—often reaching 20 to 35 percent of the congregation's annual giving, rather than the 8 to 15 percent in smaller churches."[5]

Sometimes this takes the form of funding for denominational mission. Only one mile from one another, Village Presbyterian, Prairie Village, Kansas, and Country Club Christian Church, Kansas City, Missouri, usually lead in giving to support their respective denominational mission budgets. Other tall-steeple congregations rank at or near the top of their denominations.

Many others pride themselves on giving not only to the denomination but also to community outreach programs. Every city has not-for-profit organizations that deal with human need. The most effective ones, whether religious or secular, usually benefit from the generosity of the city's large mainline congregations.

The Ministry of the Building

Less than two miles of Houston's Beltway 8, separate Grace Presbyterian and the Westchase Campus of First United Methodist. The hot July day I visited, hundreds of children swarmed each facility. In addition to sacerdotal responsibilities, these congregations see themselves as weekday community centers. They offer latch-key kids a safe haven. The neighborhood children know the church as a place for everything from Vacation Bible School to tae kwon do lessons.

Tall steeples use their facilities as tools for mission. During the week they function as everything from senior citizen activity centers to voting precincts. One minister read down the list of the various Twelve Step meetings that week, and concluded, "You can recover from anything in this church!"

History and circumstance lead congregations to respond to community needs in different ways. First Baptist Church, founded in 1822, moved to its present location on the growing edge of Indianapolis in 1960. This American Baptist congregation came with a vision for community service. At the time, the area had few recreational facilities for children. The church responded by purchasing an exceptionally large piece of land and dedicating much of it to soccer and baseball fields. Since basketball rules Indiana winters, First Baptist also included a large gymnasium in the building plans.

The congregation's athletics mission statement speaks of the church's commitment "to the wholesome physical and emotional development of your child." The program values developing self-esteem, learning to respect others, and discovering the value of team effort while improving physical skills. First Baptist Church employs full-time staff to oversee this program, which involves more than three thousand boys and girls, ages five through twelve, on ninety-six baseball teams, fifty-two soccer teams, sixty-six basketball teams, and ten cheerleading squads.

From the beginning, the church considered athletics an outreach to community children. The church never intended to have recreational activities for adult members.

First Baptist Church gets few new members from the children's athletic program. First Baptist Athletics is, indeed, a community ministry with costs, not a church growth tool with benefits.

The Trend from Checkbook to Hands-on

The survey results gathered during a congregation's strategic planning process were clear. Ninety-one percent of the members wanted to do "more for missions." A close examination of the responses revealed a distinction. Those over sixty wanted to give more money to the denomination. Those under forty wanted more "hands-on" service projects.

While not always a generational difference, a trend has developed. More people seek direct involvement in mission and ministry. The same folk who express impatience with local church governance and show little concern for the welfare of denominational bureaucracy prefer projects with a beginning and an end. They express less interest in check writing than in hand-dirtying. In an era where time has become as valuable as money, this trend may signify a rising, rather than declining, commitment to Christ's church.

Rare is the tall steeple that does not do at least an occasional Habitat for Humanity house. Hallway bulletin boards proudly display poster-size photos of the homes built by the congregation. One Dallas congregation reports a thousand of its members have picked up nail, apron, and hammer to participate in this ministry made famous by President Jimmy Carter. Another pastor showed me photographs of a bare foundation and a fully completed three-bedroom home. He explained, "Our folks built this—from concrete slab to handing the keys to a needy family—in one very long week." Building and rehabilitating housing for the community's poor ignite a core of energy and excitement in many congregations. Mission Team projects enjoy great support because they combine the appeal of hands-on service with travel. The largest congregations can do as many as twenty mission trips annually. These can be as domestic as conducting a Vacation Bible School at a sister church within driving distance to as exotic as building a children's library in the shadow of Mayan ruins in the rain forest of Central America.

Circumstances determine mission possibilities. Some city congregations operate food kitchens. Suburban churches send volunteers to help staff the urban food kitchens. Some congregations partner with inner-city schools to provide tutoring. Others combine checkbook with hands-on opportunities. These range from supplying volunteers for a community center to providing services for health clinics to teaching English as a Second Language classes to assisting with welfare and Medicare forms to assisting with income tax preparation.

Tom Osborne, retired football coach at the University of Nebraska, belongs to Saint Mark's Church in Lincoln. His lifelong passion for young people led him to start a mentoring program called TeamMates. This ministry utilizes volunteers from the church to develop relationships with needy middle school students. These vulnerable-aged kids long for adults who will treat them with respect and a loving attitude. The sixth- through eighth-graders greatly benefit. However, the seventy to eighty adult participants claim they receive the greatest blessing.

The vision of Christ Church, Fort Lauderdale, Florida, includes striving to relieve suffering in the name of Jesus. To implement that vision, the church feeds four hundred to eight hundred people each Tuesday at its food kitchen as well as owns and operates a shelter for homeless families.

Since the church requires attendance at the "church of your choice," a number of those given a meal or a place to stay also worship regularly at Christ Church. God must smile when the heavily medicated mentally ill mingle with those wearing expensive silk suits to form a faith community singing "Glorious Things of Thee Are Spoken."

Houston's First Presbyterian Church sponsors the Nehemiah Center. This inner-city community house offers opportunity for both checkbook and hands-on ministry. The church not only includes it in its budget, but many members of this congregation volunteer at the center and work under the direct supervision of the center's academic staff.

Congregations frequently receive unexpected benefits from community outreach projects. First Presbyterian Church recently subscribed a $15 million capital campaign. In addition to significant expansion of the main church campus, $500,000 was designated to renovate the Nehemiah Center. Vic Pentz, the church's senior minister, claimed many members of First Presbyterian thought the gift to the Nehemiah Center was the most exciting part of the campaign.

As Pentz put it, "I believe the enthusiasm for the Nehemiah Center accounts for the success of our campaign. People get excited by what we do there." That should be expected. As Christians mature spiritually, they grow in their desire to put faith into action.

Developing Entrepreneurs of Mission

A congregation proudly displays its mission statement on a brass plaque kept in the sanctuary: "An open community of Christians gathering to seek, celebrate, live, and share the love of God for all creation." The senior minister explained that they keep it in the sanctuary because the mission statement leads this congregation. "We want decisions made, not in keeping with wishes of the ordained clergy or lay leaders, but in accordance with the mission. We want the questions to be: 'What would an open community of Christians do?' 'Are we sharing the love of God?' 'Is this in the best interest of all creation?' "

Insisting that the mission statement leads the congregation creates an atmosphere that encourages people to get involved in the mission of the church. Congregants are encouraged—"If it fits into the mission of the church, do it." The staff is pushed—"If you have a passion for a ministry, do it."

Setting people free to respond to the gifts given by God gets surprising and wonderful results. At St. Luke's in Indianapolis, Grace Nunery, a laywoman, felt called to start a church for the deaf. Attendance at the specially designed worship service attracts one hundred non-hearing people weekly.

The Reverend Dr. Linda McCoy, staff member at the same congregation, had a passion for ministry to the unchurched. Set free to pursue her vision for mission, she started an off-site worship service in a dinner theater. Called "The Garden," the service features a fourteen-piece band and draws five hundred worshipers from among the city's unchurched and anti-church population.

The pastor of a different congregation told of a church member finding a need and filling it. A young man noted that the homeless do not have phone numbers; this hampers communication efforts to assist them. With no permanent address and no personal phone number, the homeless have difficulty applying for benefits and jobs. Obviously, giving the address or phone number of the Salvation Army shelter as one's own impresses few potential employers.

This church member used the entrepreneurial spirit that

serves him well in business and applied it to mission. He secured a $20,000 grant from the mission fund of the congregation for an electronic answering system. This makes it possible for each homeless person to have a personal phone number and answering service that can be checked from any pay phone. The homeless can leave thirty-second messages—"I can't come to the phone right now. Leave a message. I'll get right back to you." Although it has the potential for abuse, this answering system offers dignity and builds self-esteem for a group of people desperately in need of both.

Mainline Core Identity: A Passion for Mission

One senior minister told me, "I believe a critical mass, like the church, can change the mentality of a society. Consequently, my vision is to renew the church for the transformation of the world. If the church doesn't do it, who will?"

That minister touched an important distinction in mainline understandings. Nearly all the tall steeples I surveyed gather the faith community around the call to transforming mission rather than theological homogeneity. This realization caused me to reassess referring to mainline faith communities as "low commitment" churches.

Generally, Evangelical churches fit the definition for "high commitment." These faith communities maintain significant requirements for attendance, membership, time, and stewardship. Evangelicals expect those affiliated with their churches to agree to a specific creedal stance. In addition, members understand they are to fulfill their mission and ministry as Christians primarily by their high commitment to the work of the faith community.

"Low commitment" has been used to describe the main-

107

lines. The term gets applied to us because we generally set the requirements for membership low. We demand little when it comes to attending and giving. Our theological tolerance frequently comes across as "you can believe just about anything and belong to that church."

The tall steeples I studied seldom set theological or behavioral requirements for membership. Consequently, the "high commitment" designation does not fit well. This does not, however, necessarily make these churches "low commitment." Every mainline congregation has a cadre of highly committed members who set standards of church participation for themselves that rank with any Evangelical congregation. It is simply not part of the mainline story to set those as requirements for everyone.

In addition, mainline congregations attract highly committed people whose focus for mission and ministry lies outside as well as inside the institutional church. These people set high personal expectations for doing mission and ministry to home, family, career, school, or other helping institutions. They simply do not expect to live out their faith commitment entirely within the church. Instead of the church doing all the mission and ministry, they expect the church to prepare them for their own mission and ministry.

This distinction has led me to think of mainline congregations as "high expectation" rather than "low commitment." Members of the mainline tall steeples I studied set exceptionally high expectations for themselves and their congregation. The church, they believe, must offer inspiration, meaning, education, and guidance for the mission and ministry to which the people feel called.

Because of the membership's high expectations, the leadership of a mainline congregation must maintain high performance standards. Consequently, as discussed in chapter 6, tall-steeple mainlines renew when they demand excellence in everything they do.

108

"LOOK FOR THE DRY GROUND"

Bay Presbyterian Church
Bay Village, Ohio

More than forty years ago, Bay Village, Ohio, made the national news. An osteopathic physician named Sam Sheppard was accused, convicted, and imprisoned for the murder of his wife. Dr. Sheppard maintained his innocence until his demise a few years ago. His wife, he claimed, was murdered by an intruder. The Sheppard murder inspired the television program *The Fugitive* and the motion picture by the same name. Recently, Dr. Sheppard's son sought DNA tests on evidence. This technology was unavailable at the time of the crime and, the son argued, would demonstrate the innocence of Dr. Sheppard. After four decades, the community has wearied of the Sheppard-saga publicity. Mystery does not become this quiet Cleveland suburb.

The Bay Presbyterian Church, on the other hand, fits in Bay Village. The church building's modern brick exterior, simple but elegant sanctuary, and beautifully landscaped parking lot belong in this community of single-family homes and tree-lined streets.

The city maintains a park directly across Lake Road from the church. This dedicated green space provides benches, a beach, and a panorama of Lake Erie. What a beautiful place to stop and appreciate the recovering health of a once-dying Great Lake. Both Bay Presbyterian and Lake Erie, on whose shore the church stands, model how renewal comes by doing the right things in the right way.

All sixty-five words of "The Vision of Bay Presbyterian Church" are inscribed on the wall outside the entrance to the sanctuary. Only the illiterate and unobservant can escape knowing that this faith community seeks to become a more inviting, Christ-centered church.

In order to be certain it translates the vision into reality, the congregation plans and evaluates regularly. Recently, over eight hundred members attended forty-three cottage meetings. Those meetings produced goals, objectives, and plans. The church publicizes its strategy for implementation extensively. This regular planning process ensures that Bay Church will not become complacent in an already significant ministry. In addition to choirs and instrumental groups, strong Bethel Bible study, and large Stephen Ministry, nearly one thousand members of the congregation participate in small groups. The church programs everything from gatherings for those who seek after discipleship to a multitude of special interest classes called "Tune In Tuesday."

Bay Presbyterian offers wide choices in worship styles. On Saturday nights, the adventuresome can experience a high-energy service of praise, prayer, and fellowship. In this gathering people are invited to sit, stand, clap, or raise their hands. Sundays begin with an old-fashioned gospel hymn sing and preaching session at 7:45 A.M. A contemporary service with full orchestra and choir follows at 9:45. A more traditional worship concludes the morning at 11:00. Hu Auburn came to the church more than twenty-two years ago after a greatly adored predecessor died of a sudden heart attack. At the time, Auburn was twenty-nine years old and had four years of experience. Fortunately for

110

all concerned, he also had a rare combination of pastoral warmth and administrative skills. Upon arriving in Bay Village, he listened to the people, heard their story, then led them through a time of healing. Vision and plan for mission came after the people trusted. Auburn downplays the notion that he has done anything particularly innovative at Bay Presbyterian. He describes his leadership style by saying, "I tell the people, 'Be like Moses. Look for the dry ground. Pay attention to what God is making possible for us.' "

When asked to account for the many worship, ministry, and mission innovations, he said, "This congregation always had a solid evangelical theology. I did not come to shift the theology. Small groups were already in place. The entire history of the church has been one of 'relational theology.' I simply kept things going in the same direction."

He continued by explaining that there was little opposition to introducing changes in worship because the people were accustomed to the more evangelical music, the spontaneity, and the informality required by contemporary worship.

Bay Presbyterian Church has found the dry ground. The congregation experiences all-time highs in membership and worship attendance. Both the church and its senior minister feel as though the best years are yet to come.

Renewal Takes More Than Praise Music and Small Groups

Some will credit renewal at Bay Presbyterian Church to sound business management practices. They will say, "Their highly competent leadership offers compelling vision, exciting plans, and effective procedures. This keeps the faith community focused on ministry and mission."

Certainly, one cannot deny that effective leadership and sound management contribute to the health of Bay Presbyterian. In fact, competent leadership practiced sound management in every vital tall steeple I surveyed. On the other hand, it takes more than good administration to flourish. All vital congregations may be well-managed, but sound management does not ensure congregational vitality. Continuing renewal benefits from a good strategic plan and a well-written *Policy and Procedure* manual. The plan and policy alone do not, however, create vitality. Well-managed local congregations sometimes close due to lack of interest.

Others will say Bay Presbyterian stays strong because it "follows the high-commitment megachurch methodology. This includes an evangelical theology, praise worship alternatives, and community life built around small groups. Every mainline church expecting renewal needs to 'go and do likewise.' "

Several congregations I surveyed effectively renew by implementing procedures developed at the non-denominational megachurches. In Lincoln, Nebraska, Cecil Bliss said, "We have studied Willow Creek, Saddleback, and others and adopted many of their ways." Consequently, the church does six weekly worship services. These include three contemporary, one traditional, one blended, and a Wednesday night Country-western Seeker service led by a "really good band." Let it be said that Lincoln's Saint Mark's United Methodist Church offers a worship experience for every taste.

Every congregation does not, however, renew by megachurch methods. In fact, a majority of the congregations I surveyed find both comfort and effectiveness in the traditional mainline worship paradigm—pipe organ, robed choirs and ministers, standing for the doxology, singing from the hymnal, and never applauding the anthem. Others report that their attempts to introduce contemporary worship have less than stellar results. As one pastor put it, "That service is not hitting it out of the park." The people attracted to these congregations, young and old alike, seem to prefer traditional ways.

Some of the vital mainlines that have had success at introducing contemporary worship as an alternative service express concerns about how to assimilate the people it attracts. Succinctly stated, the contemporary service suggests the congregation has a very different faith story than the one believed by those who attend the traditional service.

One lead pastor illustrated the assimilation dilemma. He visited their new alternative service. The associate minister, who leads the service, asked him to retrieve a microphone from a back pew. The senior minister attempted to comply with the request during the time of high-energy praise singing. A visitor clobbered the senior minister on the head with the flag she was waving as she sang. He explained, "Presbyterian ministers do not expect to be hit by flagpoles during worship. The experience is incongruous with 'decently and in good order.' "

Frankly, many mainline congregations I studied find the constituency attracted by their architecture and reputation prefer the traditional. The changes these congregations

113

make in adapting to today's expectations include quickening the pace of worship, encouraging more participation with less opportunity to be a mere spectator, and offering a wider range of excellent music. Some replace the hymnals with video screens dropped in front of stained-glass windows. Most do not.

That Which Cuts Across All Vital Churches

Vital tall steeples decide the style of worship and develop their program not on what others find effective, but on what makes sense in their setting. They concern themselves more with understanding their story and writing a new chapter in it than following the latest trends. Depending on identity, history, and expectations, that may lead to contemporary or traditional worship. A congregation might decide to accompany worship with a three-piece band or, as one United Church of Christ did, spend $1.7 million on a new organ. The congregation might decide to do more weekday small groups, or it might add traditional adult Sunday school classes. The congregation may resolve to become a high-commitment church. It may not. Mainline congregations renew by doing that which is indigenous to their local faith community. They find generic formulas inadequate.

Several factors do, however, cut across styles of worship and program. None of the vital tall steeples I surveyed mastered all of these, but they sought to adhere to the "Four *I*'s of Renewal": intimacy, inspiration, integrity, and infinite.

Intimacy: Where People Feel They Belong

All friendly churches may not be vital, but all vital churches offer friendship. They welcome visitors by mak-

114

ing them feel they belong. In these communities of intimacy, those who have been members for years often report that they go to church with all their best friends. People leave worship reminded that they are God's loved and loveable, accepted and acceptable children.

Some of these tall-steeple churches approach the size of a small city, yet provide an opportunity to experience belonging. They practice Christian hospitality by organizing to help people experience God's grace.

Inspiration: The Church of "What's Happening Now"

It happened on two different occasions. After completing an interview at one of the vital tall steeples, I stopped at nearby congregations of my own denomination. In both cases I knew the churches struggled with declining numbers and waning enthusiasm.

The comparisons were stark. On a weekday, the hallways of the vital congregations filled with children and adults. Classrooms buzzed with Bible study, aerobics for senior citizens, and three-year-olds learning "Jesus Loves Me." Signs in the parking lot directed visitors to open doors that led to the sanctuary and church offices. Even congregations in urban high-crime neighborhoods find ways to make their buildings accessible to God's people.

At the declining churches I visited, the parking lots were empty. So little activity took place, the staff locked every door into the building. For assistance, I rang doorbells and talked to administrative staff through speaker systems. In one case, even after I explained my mission and identity, no one ever came to the door. The lack of weekday activity does not cause these congregations to decline. It is, however, symptomatic.

By definition, vivacity marks the vital congregations.

People go to these churches for the same reason a house fly goes to honey. They find life-giving energy. Whether contemporary, traditional, or blended, worship expresses the spiritual vitality that emanates from an authentic belief in and search for God. Even though the ministers settle in different places along the theological spectrum, each preaches with the theological fire of sincere belief. Some choirs sing Bach, and others sing praise choruses. None, however, think of their music as "performance." These choirs lead worship by singing *a gloria dei*.

Leaders plan participatory, authentic, high-energy worship experiences. Hymns, Scriptures, litanies, prayers, and sermons flow seamlessly. Well-prepared participants make a conscious effort to eliminate "dead spots." This keeps the service moving and energized. These congregations intend for people to leave inspired—filled with the breath of life.

Integrity: Make It Pervade Everything

The vital congregation sets a priority for placing integrity at the heart of everything the church does. Both the preaching and the programs seek to model theological authenticity. The church wants to create an atmosphere in which congregants trust staff, and staff trust the congregation. Followers allow leaders to make decisions because the leadership values the opinions of followers.

Needless to say, many fall short of fully actualizing this. Vital congregations have their share of problems, conflicts, and disappointments. Some congregations have terminated clergy for inappropriate behavior. Some members of these congregations have been known to behave in unacceptable ways. Striving to live out their faith and life together with integrity is, however, a priority.

Infinite: To Take a Peek at Ultimate Reality

Vital faith communities not only buzz with activity, they cry out, "Surely the presence of the Lord is in this place." This happens because these faith communities empower structures of meaning. Their constituency believes pulpit and program offer an authentic proclamation of what God has done in Christ Jesus. The theology makes meaningful their experience as children, parents, spouses, workers, and citizens. The church offers hope for a seeker's spiritual journey by providing direction and encouragement for the times of grief, divorce, and disappointment.

In his well-known sermon of a generation ago, "Why People Come to Church," Leslie Weatherhead contended they come to worship God, to find fellowship, to be forgiven, and to seek strength for daily life. That has not changed. People still come for the same reasons. They return because they find what they had been seeking. On occasion the reward goes well beyond the ordinary. A little corner of reality is lifted, and they catch a glimpse of the Kingdom.

LIVING OUT A NEW DAY

Christ Church United Methodist

Fort Lauderdale, Florida

Commercial Boulevard intersects U.S. Highway 1 at a busy South Florida crossroads. High-rise office buildings, car dealerships, and an array of businesses and chain restaurants fan out along those streets for miles. Traffic creeps along, often mimicking a six-lane parking lot. A few blocks to the north of the intersection sprawls the campus of D. James Kennedy's evangelical megachurch, Coral Ridge Presbyterian. An imposing two-hundred-foot, cross-topped steeple declares its presence.

Less than a hundred yards from Commercial and Highway 1, Christ Church United Methodist is tucked behind an office building and parking deck. Only the sign in the grassy field used for Sunday parking directs the visitor to the church down a side street in a residential neighborhood. The facility typifies warm-climate architecture. Outdoor walkways lined with an abundance of flowers connect several functional buildings to make a lovely setting.

An unguided walking tour sends a message of vitality. Bulletin boards offer long lists of upcoming social and educational events. Flyers advertise mission opportunities.

Hallways bustle with adults coming and going. Laughing children, wearing the uniforms of Christ Church's private elementary school, play kickball in the outdoor recreation area. A sign directs clients to the church's counseling center.

Christ Church offers a variety of weekend worship opportunities. They begin on Friday night with a "Recovery Service" for people involved in Twelve Step programs. The senior pastor explained that this service started as a way "to name the higher power for the people in AA who regularly meet in the church." This service of praise is attended regularly by eighty people. On Saturday night, a four-piece band and six singers headline a contemporary service held in the church gymnasium. The night I attended, one hundred seventy-five casually dressed people sang praise choruses projected from a computer onto screens. The senior pastor preached a tender message of God's love, liberally sprinkled with illustrations from his personal life. Before the weekend was over, he was to preach that sermon three more times.

The Sunday schedule begins at 6:30 A.M. with a time for prayer. The congregation's lay leadership gathers with the paid staff to pray for those who lead the morning services. The order for this worship regularly includes lay leadership and clergy wandering the sanctuary and gymnasium to pray for the needs of the people who will be sitting in those places later in the morning.

Simultaneous services are conducted at 9:30. In the gymnasium, the contemporary music team again brings out the band instruments, screens, and computer presentation software to lead a praise service. The crowd of two hundred fifty tends to be young adults and youth. At the same time, the largest crowd of the weekend gathers in the sanctuary. Although called "contemporary," the service experiences more as "blended" worship. Its heavy emphasis on

119

nineteenth-century gospel music may explain why the five hundred to six hundred people who gather fit the demographic expectations for South Florida.

United Methodist traditionalists can feel at home in Christ Church at 11:00. That service looks much the same as it did forty years ago. Acolytes process with a robed choir. Musical selections blend classical anthems with traditional hymns and contemporary choruses. I noted with interest that the four hundred worshipers present included many young families. One can only assume some young adults prefer traditional Methodist liturgy over a free-form contemporary style. Although the variety of worship opportunities says something significant, a full understanding of Christ Church requires an examination of what happens at times other than Sunday morning. Each week, eight hundred to nine hundred church members gather in one of one hundred Wesley Fellowship Groups for prayer, fellowship, accountability, and Bible study. The congregation owns and operates housing for the homeless, as well as an inner-city kitchen that feeds four hundred to eight hundred people each Tuesday. Many congregants participate actively in those outreach programs.

In a marked departure from the denominational standard, Christ Church has abandoned regular governance by Administrative Board in favor of leadership by consecrated lay pastors. These ministers come from the congregation's membership. Some fulfill requirements of United Methodist polity by leading the Finance Committee, the Trustees, or the Pastor-Parish Relations Committee. Others facilitate Wesley Fellowship Groups. Still others oversee action ministries, such as a music team or one of the outreach projects. As a condition of their consecration, lay pastors accept four responsibilities: (1) to pray and read Scripture daily; (2) to begin each function they lead with prayer; (3) to write a monthly report on their ministry; (4) to attend the monthly meeting of lay ministers.

Dick Wills, the senior pastor who supervises the lay pastors, accounted for the evolution of this new form of governance by saying, "I notice there is only one place in the Bible where people voted on anything. In Acts 27, they voted to cast off from shore in the face of a storm. The boat sank! I went to the Administrative Board and told them the Bible offered little encouragement for voting. They agreed. A year or two later, the question was asked, 'If we don't vote, why do we meet?' I told them that if they didn't want to meet, I saw no reason to do so. Today, the Administrative Board meets only once each year."

He continued by telling how the lay-pastor concept took hold at Christ Church: "I also noticed in 1 Peter 5 there seemed to be a lot of pastors present in the early church. We decided we should do the same thing. God started calling leaders from within the church and setting them aside for a ministry. Now we have one hundred twenty-five lay pastors."

My first impression of this congregation was, "This is not your traditional United Methodist Church. Christ Church, Fort Lauderdale, represents an evolving new species." Closer study, however, convinced me it has simply written an imaginative next chapter in a story consistent with the movement started by John Wesley. Certainly, Dick Wills, senior pastor for more than a decade, believes the congregation has renewed, not reinvented itself. "Most vital churches," he noted, "come into being in one of two ways: (1) a new church starts at the edge of town, in a vacant lot; or (2) an existing congregation is pounded down to a few members and then rebuilt from the ground up. We are doing what is seldom done. This congregation is genuinely renewing. We are, obviously, not a new church start, and we did not drive out the majority of our members in order to start fresh."

According to Dick Wills's account, Christ Church was founded in 1958 and had remarkable growth through the 1960s and into the 1970s. The retirement of the long-tenured, dearly loved pulpiteer who built the church extracted a heavy toll in numbers. There followed a series of ministerial changes. At one point, the congregation had three senior pastors in four years. During that time, the church held together around a strong classical music program led by a highly competent and deeply loved lay deacon. His unexpected departure from the staff in late 1985 sent shock waves through the faith community.

Dick Wills was appointed to Christ Church in mid-1986. Even though he found the congregation angry and divided, their numbers held. Twenty-five hundred people still claimed membership. Wills reports that for five years, he applied every renewal technique in the mainline minister's arsenal. Little of significance happened.

The turnaround began with a visit to South Africa for a Methodist World Evangelism event. The joy of the local people overwhelmed him. "Those people owned little but possessed great joy," he recalled. "Americans have many possessions but not nearly the joy." The satisfaction experienced by South Africans came, Wills concluded, from a faith that grew from the Wesley Fellowship Group meetings they regularly attended.

Several months after returning to Fort Lauderdale, Wills recommended that the congregation bring a South African minister to teach Christ Church about Wesley Fellowship Group meetings. The lay leaders agreed. An African minister came to spend six months with them. When he left, twenty small groups were in place. From those small groups, spiritual renewal began to bubble. As the senior minister puts it, "I have not always known where things were going. It has been like building a bridge as you cross the bridge." To define a clear understanding of what God wanted for Christ Church, Wills went on a personal prayer retreat. He returned to advocate what he believed God had given him:

The Vision of Christ Church

1. To introduce people to Jesus in positive ways.
2. To disciple believers through Wesley Fellowship Groups.
3. To relieve suffering.

A year after sharing this vision, the church accepted this as its vision statement. Today, the statement is printed on the front of every week's bulletin and undergirds all program planning. In addition, candidates for membership are queried as to their willingness to support the vision of the congregation.[1]

Mainline Congregations Can Renew; They Have Done It Before

My study led me to conclude that an established mainline congregation renews when intentional, high-expectation leadership works within the congregation's historical understanding of itself to plan for and sustain a vital faith community where mission is clear and worship as well as programs are indigenous to the life of the congregation.

Christ Church meets each of these criteria. The church has a vital community where people gather in the hopes of catching a glimpse of Ultimate Reality. The committed, intentional leadership offers a vision of where the congregation heads and a plan for how to get there. The church maintains a standard of excellence. Congregants expect their worship and program to be indigenous, that is, meaningful to their constituency. As common among mainliners, Christ Church does not try to force its membership to believe the same things in the same way. Instead of emphasizing the need for walking in theological lockstep, this congregation organizes around a common commitment to the vision it believes God has given Christ Church.

Christ Church has been transformed. It used to be a very traditional congregation sliding toward decline. This faith community now has a style of mission and ministry that may set the new century's standard for mainline vitality. Christ Church, Fort Lauderdale, lives out an imaginative new chapter in the congregation's story. It has become the next generation of a faith community founded more than forty years ago.

Renewal: A Process with a Long History

Circumstances change continually. The expectations and perceptions of people change. Past performance never guarantees future success. What the last generation found meaningful, the next often judges irrelevant. Consequently, every congregation that conducts a vital ministry in more than one generation has found some way to renew. Revitalizing mainlines seems new to us, but the process has a long history.

The written accounts about Center Church, New Haven, and Second Presbyterian Church, Indianapolis, suggest congregations renew through centuries in much the same way they renew into the next decade. Revitalization comes when the congregation makes its sacred story relevant to the changed circumstances by writing a new chapter. This renewed self-understanding functions as the operating system into a different generation. The new chapter provides familiar links to the church's past and offers vision to pull the community into the future. Effectively written new chapters resonate with current members' understanding of their faith journeys as well as attract a sufficient number of the next generation to keep the congregation viable for mission and ministry.

Center Church
New Haven, Connecticut
Founded 1638

In the spring of 1638, English Puritans led by the Reverend John Davenport founded Center Church.[2] In doing so, they perceived themselves on a great errand to redeem not only the New Haven colony but also the world. With

125

covenantal theology, ecclesiastical discipline, and evangelical fervor, this congregation set out to be the culture-shaping force in the community.[3] Although the name came from their location at the center of the New Haven green, the church thought of itself as residing at the community's spiritual as well as geographic center.[4] This basic way of thinking about Center Church and its mission settled into place with the founding generation.

In an in-depth, longitudinal study of the congregation, Harry Stout and Catherine Brekus report that by Center Church's three hundred fiftieth anniversary in 1989, seventeen ministers, spanning a dozen generations of parishioners, had conducted worship on 18,252 consecutive weeks. In that time, the congregation had gone through numerous times of both growth and decline. Revitalization, Stout and Brekus report, "is an old story whose roots go back to the colonial era."[5] The congregation's cyclical pattern of rise and decline can be correlated not only to outside changes in culture and community, but also to Center Church's ability to adapt to changing times while maintaining a persistent belief in the congregation's religious and historical importance.[6]

Nearly every generation at Center Church challenged something about the congregation's ways of thinking and doing. Consequently, every generation added a chapter by reframing some dimension of the original story. As a Puritan church in colonial times, Center Church struggled through issues ranging from whether children of founders should be accepted as members on the faith of their parents;[7] to whether conversion might be instantaneous or must be gradual; to the growing numbers and changing role of women in the church.[8] Throughout the colonial period, even though they changed to accommodate those issues, congregants maintained their original understanding of Center Church's mission as a Puritan church to be

"People of the Word," bound in covenant to God, and dispatched on a great errand in the wilderness.

The American Revolution Shakes Puritan Foundations

This vision guided the congregation for nearly a century and a half. Then came the American War of Independence. That spat with the British proved to be far more than a political disagreement. Puritan Center Church found individualism, voluntary associations as repositories of personal values and meaning, and the separation of church and state as well as other radical ideas from the Revolution alien to its mission.[9]

After the War of Independence, a new, competing set of congregations came to New Haven. Center Church lost its religious monopoly. Protestant newcomers, particularly the Baptists and Methodists, offered understandings of the Christian faith more congenial to the ideals of the new republic than traditional Puritanism. In 1818, Congregational Churches of Connecticut lost "establishment" status. Center Church no longer received tax support as the "official religion" of New Haven. After that, Center Church could no longer presume to have sole charge of community moral and spiritual life.[10] Its members lost their privileged place in New England society. Central themes from their founding story had been dislodged.

For the next few decades, congregation vitality relied on the strength of the leaders and the fact that each generation of children followed their parents into membership. The post-Revolutionary church maintained slow numerical growth until America's westward migration lured the younger generation of its pillar families. This meant Center Church could no longer depend on refilling the pews by biological reproduction. The original Puritan vision no longer sustained them. To renew into the next century, the church needed a new way to think about mission and ministry.

Puritanism with a Yankee Twist

Between 1806 and 1822 two powerful preachers renewed the congregation by recasting the old Puritan theology into an imaginative new chapter of the congregation's story.[11] These leaders began to celebrate self-reliance, free will, and self-determination as though doing so constituted an extension of colonial Puritanism. This appealed to citizens of the new American republic. In addition, the preaching at Center Church harmonized with the revivalism of the era by emphasizing individual conversion.

These changes renewed the faith community. By the middle of the nineteenth century "more people than ever were becoming members."[12] In 1860, the church offered three services on Sunday, plus an array of other weekday activities. Mid-nineteenth-century Center Church became the programmatic prototype of the seven-day-a-week church. During this time, the ministers managed to keep peace in the congregation on the controversial issue of that era by employing the "I can certainly agree with you on one point" strategy that is still used by clergy today. On the hot topic of slavery, ministers informed the congregation of its mutually complementary antislavery and anti-abolitionist views. To be certain they covered all bases, these politically skilled pastors also endorsed a cause widely supported in the congregation—establishing a colony for freed slaves in Africa.[13]

Center Church weathered the eighteenth- and nineteenth-century social and cultural upheavals by making significant change in its self-understanding. At the congregation's bicentennial, the minister outlined a carefully revised Puritan past to make it fit the Yankee present. Parts of the original story that did not fit present circumstances—such as civic intolerance, state tax support, and strict discipline—were shrugged off or ignored. The Puritan demand for a tight covenantal community was abandoned in favor of the new republicanism and the American way of life.[14]

To the congregation at that time, it sounded like the next generation of the ideas brought to New Haven by the founders. Although significantly reconstructed, Center Church still envisioned itself as being on a great errand to shape a Christian society.[15] The membership felt justified in continuing the belief in the congregation's religious and historical importance.

The Struggle to Renew into a New Millennium

Through the nineteenth century, Center Church managed to remain in the spiritual heart of the community. In the view of Stout and Brekus, that ceased in the twentieth century when the congregation lost its identity as a spiritual institution at the center of New Haven.[16] Several factors contributed. The competition for members grew geometrically, as many different religious groups started churches. The population of New Haven became racially and ethnically diverse. The theological gap between the pulpit and pew steadily widened with the rise of theological liberalism.

The leadership of Center Church failed to find a meaningful way to meet these challenges. As their traditional constituency shrank, they made no significant effort to evangelize the changing population. The new liberal theol-

129

ogy movement, in which Center Church's ministers held positions of national prominence, had refreshing ways to reconcile science and religion for educated seekers but showed little evidence of appealing to inner-city audiences.[17]

Whereas earlier generations of ministers revised Puritan history and principles to fit changing needs and circumstances, twentieth-century leaders chose to disparage the revivalism, conversionism, and pietism of their heritage.[18] The social reforming impulse of the Puritan past remained. However, it was cut off from the personal spiritual needs of the congregants. Social issues became ends unto themselves.[19]

Over the next few decades, the lack of a compelling vision extinguished the energizing portions of Center Church's sacred story. The congregation no longer perceived itself as on a great errand to shape New Haven culture and values. The church that once resided at the spiritual center of the community drifted to the margin.

The persistent belief in Center Church's religious and historical importance remained, but only as a radical restatement of what that meant to previous generations. Instead of being important, by mid-twentieth century, the goal became preserving the memory of being important. In the 1920s the church began to open its doors for tourist groups to visit the building and its crypts. This symbolized the beginning of Center Church's slide from doing ministry into becoming a museum. In cutting themselves off from missional, outreaching, evangelizing elements of their past, congregants reduced the church's sacred story to something that had little appeal to a critical mass of the New Haven population.[20]

On October 27, 1989, Center Church celebrated its three hundred fiftieth anniversary. A congregation of sixty-eight people, most past retirement age, gathered for the celebration in a sanctuary designed to seat one thousand.[21] For more than a dozen generations, this congregation renewed through war and social upheaval. Now it faced the possibility of not having a viable mission and ministry into its four hundredth anniversary.

Center Church has experienced some turnaround in the past decade. Numbers are still small, but a younger generation has joined the membership ranks. Worship attendance hovers around one hundred. Although past performance does not guarantee future success, this faith community may turn it around. Center Church has done it many times.

Second Presbyterian Church
Indianapolis, Indiana
Founded 1838

Second Presbyterian Church has the look of a modern Gothic cathedral. Its Indiana limestone building dominates its North Meridian Street neighborhood, just a few miles from the downtown area. Everything about the church speaks of its expectation for excellence. The halls on weekdays bustle with children and adults. Bulletin boards announce an abundance of spiritual-growth activities and mission opportunities. Worship and Sunday school attendance statistics indicate the church has been on a steady growth incline for more than a decade. The vision statement regularly appears in publications, and the church operates with a plan for accomplishing it. This faith community runs on a track that will take it well into the new century with vitality.

Like Center Church in New Haven, Second Presbyterian Church has been through the renewal process many times. In its first few years, it grew to be the state's largest Presbyterian church. It also acquired an early reputation for providing business and political and civic leaders to the city. For seventeen decades, the congregation has found a way to renew continually and maintain the reputation as a tall-steeple church that provides community leadership.

In reading George Geib's history of Second Church,[22] I was struck by how often he describes renewal though continuous rather than discontinuous change. To use my metaphor, not Geib's, the congregation changed by writing new chapters. At times continuity required great imagination. For instance, irrational, unlettered revivalism bothered Henry Ward Beecher, the congregation's most well-known minister. The revival-meeting style of preaching was sweeping the frontier. Its unfettered enthusiasm attracted crowds, but it ran contrary to Second Church's reasoned approach to the Reformed faith. In spite of finding the style offensive, Beecher recognized its popularity. He had to admit it brought people into church. This innovative pastor studied and experimented with the style. Eventually, he found a way to blend its enthusiastic presentation with a well-thought-out message of biblical truth and confessional consistency.[23] From then on, Second Church heard Beecher preach thoughtful, traditional Presbyterianism like a revivalist.

Henry Ward Beecher pioneered experimenting with worship and ministry. He developed a strategy for incorporating something new without doing disservice to traditional, dignified Presbyterian ways. Second Church learned that lesson well.

Many mainline churches today feel pressed to attempt alternative styles of worship. Many respond by introducing forms of worship not in keeping with their traditions. Rather than attempt the route of praise choruses with a rock band, Second Presbyterian applied the Beecher strategy. After an extensive study of effective mainline alterna-

132

tive worship styles, the congregation introduced a more casual, highly participatory Sunday evening service, preached by the senior minister. While not praise choruses, the music is contemporary and presented by the church's finest musicians. This satisfies the call for an alternative service, but keeps with the Second Church standards of informed and dignified worship.

The founding generation established the nature of this congregation. The fundamental constructs they put in place still shape the faith community's understanding of mission and ministry. Since the mid-1840s, Second Church has been known as

1. A Presbyterian "preacher's church." Second Church has always emphasized its Reformed heritage. Beecher's sermons set a high standard in preparation and presentation. Great preaching still holds the congregation together.
2. A church that does the basic work of congregational life well. This requires committed, competent lay leaders who work through effective governance to provide both outstanding physical facilities and educational programs. Second Church has never lost sight of the importance of ecclesiastical nuts and bolts.
3. An urban church. Second Church was founded in a rapidly growing city. Early on, members realized the church had an important leadership role to play in the community. Present commitment to urban issues continues that part of the story.[24]

For Second Presbyterian Church, renewal is continual. Like many mainline congregations, Second Church just does it. May its tribe increase.

133

JUST DOING THE JOB WELL

Saint John United Church of Christ

Saint Charles, Missouri

Eighteenth-century French traders founded Saint Charles, Missouri. The community once served as the state capital. Today the urban sprawl of Saint Louis encompasses the community.

Saint John Church stands on the hill overlooking Saint Charles's restored historic district. Since 1869, the functional red brick building has undergone numerous expansions and renovations. Its German founders intended to build a pleasant place for ordinary folks to worship, not a cathedral. They succeeded.

The congregants continue that tradition of steadfastness in lieu of the spectacular. They specialize in doing mission and ministry well. Their spotless building fits with the manicured flower beds. Traditional worship and Christian nurture opportunities feed the spiritual life of the congregants.

Harv Kramme, the senior minister, attributes the congregation's strong and steady course to several factors. Saint John focuses on traditional worship done excellently. The congregants offer warm hospitality to visitors and deliver effective pastoral care to members. They budget 22 to 23 percent of their giving to outreach causes. The church puts particular emphasis on music for the youth. In fact, Saint John has a 1950s-styled youth music program that draws from the entire city. Kramme also believes the outstanding, long-tenured staff, three with more than twenty years' service, adds to the stability of congregational life.

I believe this church also benefits significantly from Harv Kramme's leadership. He reports that when he came twenty-one years ago, he realized the congregation needed to establish a more meaningful ministry identity in the community. He got the idea of becoming known as the church in town with the best children's music program. As an effective leader, he also understood the importance of writing a new chapter in the congregation's history and not a new story. "I sold the congregation on the need to continue tradition," he said, "by going in a new direction."

The church has benefited from this deliberative leadership style. Kramme has the patience to build the support of the people. He also understands how to compromise when that support cannot be attained. For instance, the youth music advocates wanted to remodel the formal split chancel to make it more flexible. Older members of the congregation objected. As the senior minister explained, "I learned early in ministry to give people lots of time and input. It pays." A compromise was struck. They found a way to remodel the chancel so that it could be arranged for the occasional musical performance by the youth and then returned to the traditional split chancel for regular worship services. Constructing a marble surface on the chancel, improving the sound system, and adding several ranks to the pipe organ proved beneficial for both regular worship and occasional performance.

Saint John United Church of Christ, of course, does not hold an annual teaching seminar on innovative ministry. Its name cannot be found on the list of the nation's benchmark congregations. Indeed, it should not. Little they do can be claimed extraordinary. Instead, this church simply does ministry in a faithful, if unspectacular, way with its eighteen hundred members. These folks give about $700,000 annually to the work of Christ's church. Of that amount, about $150,000 benefits those beyond the local congregation. Two hundred children and youth continually learn the discipline of music at Saint John Church. Each week nearly six hundred come to worship in hopes of encountering Ultimate Reality. The congregation works faithfully at its ministry year after year, decade after decade.

My excitement about Saint John comes from its effectiveness at renewing as a mainline, by doing ministry in a mainline way. May the tribe of Saint John increase.

Better News Than Expected

When I proposed doing a study on how large, mainline congregations renew over long periods of time, a prominent church leader warned me, "Your study will not take long. There are not very many." I assumed that in order to fill out my three-month study leave, I might have to talk to every congregation that fit my study profile. Imagine my delight when I discovered that, even though not as abundant as a generation ago, mainline tall steeples still dot the landscape of most cities.

When I asked a denominational executive to name a few of their vigorous tall steeples still using traditional forms of worship, he said, "I can name many more who have gone to contemporary formats." From that comment I assumed the next generation of vital tall steeples either already has made or will make radical changes in the way they worship.

I did not find this assumption true. The majority I surveyed not only continue to worship in rather traditional ways, but their attempts to introduce contemporary worship frequently fizzle or have less than spectacular results. Contrary to the dire predictions of populist ecclesiastical mythology, traditional ways can attract sufficient young adults to enter the next century strong in number, mission, and ministry.

My study has significant limitations. I gathered information from only fifty congregations. My sampling methods fell short of scientific polling standards. Ethnic minority sampling is particularly small. My findings, I am convinced, apply only to mainline, predominantly Caucasian, established congregations. I am not prepared to generalize about a rosy future for mainlines of every size and circumstance. On the other hand, I am more hopeful about the future than I have been in years.

Present Trends Do Not Always Predict Future Results

In recent years news from the mainlines has not been good. Some predict the closing of one-third to as many as one-half of all mainline congregations in the next generation. If mainline Protestantism continues its same statistical rate of decline, it will disappear from the American scene in thirty-five years.

Fortunately, present trends do not always predict future results. A comedian once observed that in 1964, automobiles on the San Francisco freeways averaged 2.8 passengers. By 1975, that average dropped to 1.7 people per car. If this trend continues, by 2015 there "will be fewer than one person in each car on our freeways!" Projecting mainline extinction from present tendencies encounters the same difficulty.

A group of newly commissioned army officers sat on bleachers watching an air show of military firepower. After a half hour of strafing and bombing, the instructor assured the young second lieutenants, "In case of war, you will benefit from that support. We have the technically superior weaponry. When our air power softens them up, you can lead your troops into battle without fear of counterattack. Nothing, absolutely nothing, can survive the force you have just witnessed." As he spoke, three deer bolted from the fire-ravaged hill, crossed the road, and began to graze.

Mainline Protestantism has at least as much resiliency. These churches have been God's vehicle for taking the faith from generation to generation. I suspect that role will continue for at least another generation. As we stumble through this difficult time, let us be encouraged by good news happening in some mainline congregations. We need these stories of tall-steeple pockets of vitality. They teach lessons that apply to congregations of other sizes.

A Dinosaur Is a Dinosaur Is a Dinosaur

A vital tall steeple compares to a dinosaur: Large. Lumbering. Once the dominant species of the environment. Now slow to respond to an everchanging world.

Many of these dinosaurs have gone the way of the *Brontosaurus*. Historians of each mainline denomination provide a substantial list of the last generation's tall steeples now closed. Others, as I have demonstrated, have undergone heart transplants, recovered good health, and have an excellent prognosis.

Still, I suspect, the dinosaur comparison fits. Mainline tall steeples are as unlikely to dominate the landscape as *Tyrannosaurus rex* is to make a comeback. The same probably holds for mainline denominations in general. Indeed, a dinosaur is a dinosaur is a dinosaur.

We should not expect the total extinction of mainline American Protestant witness. Again, dinosaurs compare well; they did not totally disappear. In fact, their descendants still live among us. If the assessments of paleoanatomists can be trusted, birds represent their nearest relatives. Unlike their ancestors, birds do not dominate the environment. They do, however, make very significant contributions.

The metaphor holds. Mainline Protestantism, particularly its tall-steeple congregations, may never again dominate the culture. They will, however, transform and survive. They will make contributions as significant to culture as birds make to nature.

139

Introduction

1. William S. Worley, *J. C. Nichols and the Shaping of Kansas City* (Columbia: University of Missouri Press, 1990), p. 276.

2. This was the expression used by George Hamilton Combs, founding pastor of Country Club Christian Church, when he described his theology of pastoral ministry.

1. Where People Encounter Ultimate Reality

1. This congregation does not fit the American definition of a tall steeple. However, I was sufficiently impressed with three hundred in worship in London to include Saint Columba's in this study.

2. Donald Morgan, "How an Old Historic Church Became New," in *Good News in Growing Churches*, ed. Robert L. Burt (New York: The Pilgrim Press, 1990), pp. 144-45.

3. John Cobb, *Reclaiming the Church* (Louisville: Westminster John Knox Press, 1997), pp. 100-3.

2. Pay Heed to the Story

1. "A Time to Dream," a pamphlet announcing the formation of the St. Luke's Endowment, undated.

2. This story has many versions and interpretations. It is paraphrased here from Ernest Kurtz and Katherine Ketcham, *The Spirituality of Imperfection: Modern Wisdom from Classic Stories* (New York: Bantam Books, 1992), pp. 7-8. This interpretation, admittedly, strays from the use made of the story in Hasidic Judaism.

3. James Hopewell, *Congregation: Stories and Structure* (Philadelphia: Fortress Press, 1987), p. xii.

4. A line from the hymn "I Love Thy Kingdom, Lord." Morgan, "How an Old Historic Church Became New," in *Good News in Growing Churches*, pp. 139, 145.

5. Ibid., p. 145.

6. Hopewell, *Congregation: Stories and Structure*, p. 5.

7. Ibid., p. 7.

8. Ibid., p. xiv.

9. Ibid.

10. Ibid., p. 7.

3. Principles of Change in the Long-Established Church

1. Barry Johnson, "By Faith Together," in *Good News in Growing Churches*, p. 66.

2. Jack F. Matlock, Jr., *Autopsy on an Empire* (New York: Random House, 1995), p. 17.

3. For a discussion of theoretic foundations and practical understandings of first- and second-order change, see Paul Watzlawick, John Weakland, and Richard Fisch, *CHANGE: Principles of Problem Formation and Problem Resolution* (New York: W. W. Norton and Company, 1974), pp. 1-27.

4. From Joe Taylor Ford, *Sourcebook of Wit and Wisdom* (Canton, Ohio: Communication Resources, 1996), p. 58.

5. Ibid.

4. Renewing Congregations Have Leaders of Vision

1. James McBride, *The Color of Water* (New York: Riverhead Books, 1996), p. 202.

2. Robert L. Swigart, chair of the board, The Kollmorgen Company. Quoted in James Kouzes and Barry Posner, *The Leadership Challenge: How to Get Things Done in an Organization* (San Francisco: Jossey-Bass, 1993), p. 81.

3. Proverbs 29:18, King James Version.

4. Peter Senge, *The Fifth Discipline: The Art and Practice of the Learning Organization* (New York: Doubleday, 1990), p. 209.

5. Bert Nanus, *Visionary Leadership* (San Francisco: Jossey-Bass, 1992), p. 8.

6. Comments on "The State of the Church," General Assembly of the Christian Church, Denver, Colorado, July 1997.

7. From the autobiography of George Hamilton Combs, *I'd Take This Way Again* (Saint Louis: Bethany Press, 1944), p. 73.

8. Comments by Roy Stauffer in the Lindenwood Christian Church newsletter, April 1997.

9. Ken Callahan's *Twelve Keys to an Effective Church* (San Francisco: Harper & Row, 1983) and Herb Miller's *The Vital Congregation* (Nashville: Abingdon Press, 1990) are excellent resources.

10. John Killinger, *The Greatest Teachings of Jesus* (Nashville: Abingdon Press, 1993), p. 25.

11. Nanus, *Visionary Leadership*, p. 8.

12. Killinger, *The Greatest Teachings of Jesus*, p. 36.

5. Make It Happen

1. Richard Lynch, *LEAD!* (San Francisco: Jossey-Bass, 1993), p. 18.

2. Henry Mintzberg, *The Rise and Fall of Strategic Planning* (New York: The Free Press, 1994).

3. Leonard Sweet, "Sweet's SoulCafe," October and November 1997, p. 9.

6. Renewal Demands Excellence

1. "The Things We Have Done Together," a sermon by Frank Harrington, October 20, 1996.

2. After the completion of the manuscript for this book, I was saddened to learn of Frank Harrington's sudden and unexpected death.

3. Cobb, *Reclaiming the Church*, pp. 1-3.

7. Outreach Takes Priority in Renewing Mainlines

1. John Buchanan, *Becoming Church, Becoming Community* (Louisville: Westminster John Knox, 1996), p. 29. I read this book a full year before I began this study on renewing tall-steeple mainline congregations. It was a great source of hope. This book was the first writing I encountered that spoke positive results from applying traditional mainline methods of doing and being the church.

2. Ibid., p. xii.

3. From Peter Benson and Carolyn H. Eklin, *Effective Christian Education: A National Study of Protestant Congregations—A Summary Report on Faith, Loyalty, and Congregational Life* (Minneapolis: Search Institute, 1990).

4. Burt, *Good News in Growing Churches*, p. 138.

5. Herb Miller, personal correspondence, August 29, 1997.

9. Mainline Congregations Can Renew

1. For more on Christ Church in Fort Lauderdale, see Dick Wills, *Waking to God's Dream: Spiritual Leadership and Church Renewal* (Nashville: Abingdon Press, 1999).

2. Harry S. Stout and Catherine Brekus, "A New England Congregation, Center Church, New Haven, 1638-1989," in *American Congregations, Volume 1: Portraits of Twelve Religious Communities,* eds. James P. Wind and James W. Lewis (Chicago: University of Chicago Press, 1994), p. 18. I am deeply indebted to Stout and Brekus for their remarkable, in-depth, longitudinal study of Center Church. They are correct in contending that it offers "an accurate examination of social and intellectual change in one congregation over the whole course of American history."

3. Ibid.
4. Ibid., p. 21.
5. Ibid., p. 17.
6. Ibid., p. 18.
7. Ibid., p. 24.
8. Ibid., pp. 40-45.
9. Ibid., pp. 48-49.
10. Ibid., p. 51.
11. Ibid., pp. 52-53.
12. Ibid., p. 69.
13. Ibid., p. 70.
14. Ibid., p. 71.
15. Ibid., p. 72.
16. Ibid., p. 73.
17. Ibid., pp. 78-79.
18. Ibid., p. 77.
19. Ibid., p. 78.
20. Ibid., p. 90.
21. Ibid., p. 15.
22. George Geib, *Lives Touched by Faith* (Indianapolis: Second Presbyterian Church, 1988).
23. Ibid., p. 23.
24. Ibid., pp. 34-35.